choosing
the right
dog
for you

choosing the right dog for you

Profiles of over 200 dog breeds

Gwen Bailey

hamlyn

An Hachette Livre UK Company
First published in Great Britain in 2004 by
Hamlyn, a division of Octopus Publishing Group Ltd
2–4 Heron Quays, London E14 4JP
www.octopusbooks.co.uk

ISBN-13: 978-0-600-61017-5
ISBN-10: 0-600-61017-9

A CIP catalogue record for this book
is available from the British Library

Printed and bound in China

10 9 8 7 6 5 4 3 2

Contents

Introduction

Acquiring a new dog is one of life's true pleasures. Since dogs can live up to 15 years or more, it is very important to make the right choice of personality at the beginning. Try not to let the excitement of getting a dog blind you to the realities of life with that breed, especially when looking for a puppy.

Most of us live in close proximity to our dogs, inviting them into our homes and lives. It is therefore essential that we are compatible in as many areas as possible. Every dog is different and getting a good match between you, your family and the new dog will make it easier to live in harmony together.

The range of characteristics of pet dogs is endless. There are lively dogs that need lots of exercise, large ones that would not fit into a small flat, noisy ones that annoy the neighbours, aloof ones, and ones that want to sit on your lap all day and be cuddled. Whatever your requirements, there is usually a dog for you.

Cavalier King Charles Spaniel
(see page 183)

It is not that difficult to make the right choice. A little time and effort spent on research before you get a dog will make all the difference, especially before you visit a rescue centre with all those big, pleading, homeless eyes, or a litter of puppies with bundles of fluff just waiting to be taken home.

This book will help you to make a start and point you in the right direction for the next stage in the process of finding the right dog for you.

Unfortunately, not everyone takes such good care before they acquire a dog. Many dogs end up in rescue centres because of bad choices, or people live with difficult dogs for years, neither of them enjoying life as they should. There is nothing more uncomfortable than living with a dog that is not right for you, and it is not pleasant for the dog either. Making the wrong choice can make both of you miserable. By carefully matching your and your family's needs with the characteristics of the dogs available before you take one home, you are much more likely to choose a dog that you will own for the rest of its life.

Owning a dog is a voyage of discovery that starts with careful consideration of which dog to choose. It is an expedition that will bring you love and loyalty of a very special quality, and is a wonderful privilege that can last a lifetime. Making the right choice will lead to a happier life for both of you.

Finding the right dog for you can lead to years of pleasure and fun for both you and your dog.

All dogs are different

Wolves are the most likely ancestors of our pet dogs. Although wolves are very different from domesticated dogs, they provide a blueprint for our pets. Since our dogs show similar behaviour patterns, it is useful to look at this 'raw material' to give us an idea of why dogs are like they are.

Wolves are the blueprint for our pet dogs and help us understand why they behave as they do.

Wild ancestry

Wolves evolved to track, chase and bring down large deer-sized animals. To do this, they hunt as a pack and live in family groups with strong social bonds. These bonds are strengthened with a hierarchy system and the ability to display and understand an intricate system of body language signals. Wolves are fully equipped for their place in their environment and many of their behaviours, such as burying excess food, rolling in smelly substances, and hunting, have been handed down to our pet dogs.

When early humans began to settle in villages, waste dumps provided a new food supply. It is thought that ancestors of our domestic dogs exploited this new niche and gradually evolved into 'village dogs' with weaker jaws, reduced reactivity, reduced predatory desire, and probably less intelligence. From these 'watered-down' wolves, our modern day dogs were bred.

Dogs with jobs

People soon realized that they could affect the body shape and characteristics of their dogs by selecting which dogs were bred with each other. Since there was a variety of jobs that dogs could do to help people survive and prosper, dogs of different shapes and sizes were bred specifically for different useful activities.

For example, large dogs with thick coats were bred to help fishermen in Newfoundland haul in nets and retrieve fish; elegant dogs with spotty coats were bred to run alongside the carriages of the rich, short-faced tenacious dogs were bred to hold cattle for butchers, and small active dogs were bred to catch and kill vermin.

Border Collies have the stamina to work all day and the next day too. Careful consideration is needed before taking one into your life and home.

All dogs are different

Ancestral traits

Although many of our current dogs are now bred with the aim of winning prizes for physical attributes in the show ring, most have retained the temperament traits of their ancestors. As a result, it is very important to look at the personality of the breeds you are interested in, and to find out what they were originally bred to do, so that you can get a clear picture of the inherited desires that you may be acquiring.

Q When looking at the job your chosen breed once did, what benefits will those strong inherited traits bring to your home life and what problems may they cause?

Q Will it be acceptable if your hound takes off after a deer you see while on a walk and does not come home for hours?

Q What if your Collie chases children that come to visit?

Q Is it okay if your Newfoundland regularly plunges into your pond in the garden or the fountain in the park?

Q Will it be a problem if your Keeshound is such a good watchdog that your neighbours complain about the barking?

Dogs can be trained not to do things, but it is a lot easier if there are no strong unsuitable temperament traits and desires to battle against in the first place. Find out about the temperament traits you will be acquiring and ask yourself if you will be able to provide acceptable alternatives to these behaviours so that your dog will be content.

Since many dogs were bred for the same functions in different parts of the world, we have ended up with many different breeds, some of which were bred to do similar, but slightly different jobs.

As well as the body shape, selective breeding can also choose personality traits. Consequently dogs bred to herd are not only physically adapted for chasing, but they also have a strong inherited desire to chase which can then be honed to perfection by the trainer. Similarly, dogs bred to guard are not only large and powerful, but also have strong characters and the confidence necessary to see off a threat. When choosing a dog it is as important to bear in mind the breed's character traits as it is their physical nature.

Breed groups

For simplicity, dogs are categorized into seven different groups, according to what they were bred to do. These groups are gundogs, hounds, pastoral, terriers, toys, utility dogs and working dogs. A summary of their origins and personality traits is provided. If you are not sure which breed to choose, it may help to begin by choosing a group, and then try to narrow it down.

The groups we've chosen represent the most common categorization around the world, however, different Kennel Clubs categorize dogs in different ways. For instance, the American Kennel Club has a 'Miscellaneous' group containing six breeds which European Kennel Clubs do not have. There also maybe differences of opinion as to which dogs are in which group – in the US a Bichon Frise is classed as a 'Non-sporting' dog, but in the UK it's in the 'Toy' group.

Gundogs

Also known as 'Sporting Dogs' bred to help people hunt by flushing game, pointing to game so it can be shot, and retrieving the animals that are shot. They need to work closely with people and so are usually sociable, willing to please and easy to train. They often have a soft bite so they do not damage the game they retrieve, and their desire to use their mouths can make them great chewers when growing up.

The upside is that they also play enthusiastically with toys. This makes them more fun to be

English Setter (see page 71)

with, especially for children, and makes training easier as it gives you something else to reward them with. They usually enjoy close contact with their owners, but can be boisterous if they do not get enough exercise. Most gundogs have the energy and stamina to keep on the move all day so plenty of exercise is essential. They usually make very good dogs for an active family, as they tend to be tolerant and playful with children if raised with them.

Hounds

Hounds were bred to track and hunt prey with hunters on foot, horseback or catching up later while the dog held the animal at bay. Some were bred to bring down prey and many may not be good with small pets unless they have grown up with them. Hounds often have

deep, resounding voices to let the hunter know where they are, but they do not usually bark unnecessarily. Hounds are mostly very amiable and easy-going. They were not bred to work closely with humans so can be independent and disobedient. They are not really interested in toys and can be difficult to train, tending to run off when they see something to chase.

Most hounds were bred to live in packs and, as a result, are usually sociable and friendly to humans and other dogs. They do not mind close physical contact but they are also happy with people who prefer to be less tactile. They are usually happy to relax at home, appearing lazy when there is nothing to do, but need long, energetic walks to use up their tremendous energy and desire to run.

Bloodhound (*see page 89*)

Afghan Hound (*see page 84*)

Pastoral

The pastoral group can be roughly divided into two categories – dogs that were bred to round up flocks of sheep or herds of cattle, and dogs that were bred to live with and protect flocks of sheep (the American Kennel Club calls this group 'Herding').

Herding breeds – bred to herd domesticated animals. They are hard working and need plenty of exercise for their minds and bodies. Herding breeds are great toy-players. Their excellent hearing makes them alert, active watchdogs, but it can also result in noise phobias if they are not accustomed to loud noises early in life. Herding breeds are usually sensitive and quick to react, and can be nervous if not socialized and habituated to enough experiences as puppies. They are usually very responsive to commands once they have learned them and are easily trained. They were bred to work closely with humans and prefer to have a close, strong bond with their owner, often enjoying close physical contact with plenty of stroking and fuss. A few breeds prefer a strong bond with one person, sometimes at the expense of other people in the house.

Livestock guardians – some of the larger, more powerful breeds in the pastoral group were bred to live with flocks to protect them from wolves and other predators. They can have strong guarding instincts and need adequate socialization in order to prevent aggression. They tend to be larger with heavier coats and are less energetic and reactive than the herding dogs.

Australian Shepherd (*see page 121*)

Pyrenean Mountain Dog (*see page 143*)

All dogs are different

All dogs are different

Miniature Bull Terrier (*see page 157*)

Airedale Terrier (*see page 151*)

Terriers

Bred to catch and kill animals considered to be vermin, or for sport. Most were bred to 'go to ground' to dig out animals from their lairs and so are natural diggers. Usually small in height, they tend to have very strong predatory instincts and can be dangerous around small pets unless they have grown up with them and view them as a member of their pack. Most will chase and may injure cats unless they have been raised with them.

Terriers are usually tenacious, rough players with a hard bite, but with small mouths. They often have strong characters and a busy, excitable nature, which can be very charismatic. They are easily alerted and can make good watchdogs, although for some owners, their inclination to bark can be annoying. They are feisty and quick-tempered and tend to be aggressive first and think later if something upsets them. Aggression to other dogs is a common trait among terriers. They can be stubborn and unwilling to respond to commands unless there is something in it for them, but they are usually affectionate and outgoing and many owners enjoy their extrovert, independent nature.

Cavalier King Charles Spaniel (*see page 183*)

Dalmation (*see page 208*)

Toys

Bred to be companions. Usually small in height, most make excellent pet dogs as the working traits have mostly been bred out of them. Consequently, they are usually very agreeable, mild-mannered and enjoy companionship. They are willing to please but may not be as quick to learn or responsive as the working dogs. They are usually very keen on close contact with their owners and enjoy plenty of fuss and attention. This makes them a good choice for novice owners. Their small height makes them ideal for owners without much space, but renders them prone to health problems so check puppies and adult dogs very carefully before buying to reduce the risk of inherited diseases.

Utility dogs

A mixture of breeds that are not traditionally placed in other groups but which can often be fitted into one or other of them. Also known as 'Non-sporting dogs' they were bred to do a variety of different jobs from herding to guarding, and it is necessary to look at each breed individually to find out what traits they may have, so you can decide if they fit the requirements for your lifestyle.

All dogs are different

Finding out about your chosen breed

Once you have settled on a few breeds you are interested in, the next step is to find out more. Do this by looking on the internet, asking people who own and live with dogs of your chosen breed, and by attending some dog shows.

The big dog shows will be advertised by the Kennel Club, in the dog breed press, and on the internet, or ask any large breeder for details. At shows, you will be able to meet breeders, as well as people who show their dog but also keep it as a pet. Usually people are very willing to talk about their breed and its characteristics, although it may be best to avoid talking to them just before it is their turn in the ring. It is a good idea to ask about the downsides of owning the breed and any problems they may have had as well as finding out about all the benefits.

Variation within a breed

Although you can be reasonably sure that you will get a dog that looks and acts like the breed you have chosen, you need to be aware that there will be variations between dogs of different lines within the breed. If you look at the pedigree of various dogs from a particular breed, you will find that breeders often repeatedly select certain types or strains they like. Their puppies may, therefore, be slightly different to puppies from a breeder that selects from different stock. Some breeders will also occasionally import 'new blood' from overseas and this can bring in variations in temperament as well as slight physical differences.

Variation within a litter

As with siblings of all mammals, no two puppies in a litter are the same. Some may be confident and bold, others shy and retiring. Since they are all slightly different and it is difficult to get to know each of them in the short time you spend with them to make your choice, it makes sense to ask the breeder's advice on which one may be best suited to you and your family. If you are in doubt about the ability of the breeder, take along an experienced friend to help you or go elsewhere. If your chosen breed is rare, you may have to join a waiting list and have less choice about the puppy, in which case you may have to trust the breeder to get it right for you or be prepared to wait.

It is hard to resist the appeal of puppies, but it is important to consider what they will be like as adults.

Mongrels and crossbreds

While humans have been busy deciding on which dog to breed with which, dogs have been choosing for themselves for centuries. Since there are fewer strays these days, it is getting harder to find a true mongrel (mixture of all breeds), but there are many crossbred dogs whose parentage is a recognizable mixture of two or more breeds.

Crossbreds and mongrels usually have fewer health problems than pure breeds as the genes that cause problems are diluted by a bigger gene pool. Crossbreds are also unique as no two look or act the same. If the dog is an adult when you acquire it, you can see what you are getting. However, it is a little more difficult to predict the size, shape and nature of crossbred puppies and you often have to take a chance on what they will be like once they grow up.

Upbringing

A dog's character will be a mixture of influences from its genes and upbringing. No matter how carefully you have selected the parents of your future dog, the people who raise him and the environment in which he is brought up will heavily influence his character. Whether acquiring an adult or puppy, being careful about its upbringing will help you acquire the right kind of temperament. If you are acquiring an adult, take time to get to know that particular dog to find out if he is the right choice for you.

Socialization with other dogs is an important part of growing up and will make a real difference to future behaviour.

He may be a perfect example of his breed, but early experiences will have acted on his inherited personality traits to make him the dog he is now.

If you are getting a puppy, make sure you know how to raise him so that you can give him the best start in life (see *The Perfect Puppy* by Gwen Bailey, Hamlyn). You will need to make sure your puppy has adequate socialization with people of all ages, as well as other animals including lots of other dogs. He will also need educating and training so that he can be taught to behave well in human society. Make sure you have time in your life to ensure your puppy grows up with a good temperament and character.

Things to consider

You cannot predict the future, but is this a good time in your life to be taking on a commitment that may last 15–20 years?

Is this the right time to get a dog?

Everyone's circumstances in life change from time to time and we never know what the future will hold. However, we can usually look ahead a little way and predict what life will be like for the next 10 years. Doing this will give you a good indication of whether you will be able to fit a dog into that lifestyle or not.

Finding a dog that will get on well with all members of your family is essential.

Try asking yourself the following questions before you decide whether to get a dog, and if so, which dog you should be thinking about.

Q Are you settling down with a new partner, and planning to have children? Consider getting a dog that will accept children easily to avoid problems later on and make sure it is well socialized with children of all ages while it is still a puppy.

Q Do you already have a family and are choosing a dog? Consider how the dog may cope with isolation once the children have grown up and the adults are out at work all day.

Q Will you still have the time and energy for a dog if you are planning a family?

Q Is it likely that an elderly relative may come to live with you? Consider what kind of dog would be most appropriate then.

Try to think of any other eventualities that may befall you and choose a dog that can cope with any variations you can predict for the future.

Can you afford it?

Just like children, dogs can be more expensive than you may think once you have added up all the things that you need to buy for them. After the purchase price itself, you will need to consider the following: vaccinations, puppy training and socialization classes, food, beds, collars and leads, brushes, towels, chews, toys, veterinary insurance for the big, unexpected bills, routine vet's fees for worming, check-ups, fleaspray, neutering and kennel fees when you go on holiday.

Although dogs will be just as comfortable on a soft nest of old blankets as on the most expensive bed in the shop, there are some necessities that cannot be skimped on. Always do the sums before you take on a new dog.

Things to consider

Good insurance is useful for active dogs that could cause accidents involving others or be injured themselves.

Things to consider

Do you have the time?

It is nice to have a dog around. They provide companionship, amusement, and never-ending love and loyalty. But all this comes at a price, not just in terms of money but also in mental effort and time. Before you get a dog, think realistically about the time and energy a dog may need and how you would fit it into your already busy lifestyle.

Do you have the mental and physical energy?

Do you have the physical energy for an active, energetic dog? Dogs need regular off-lead exercise at least twice a day, frequent games to entertain and exercise them, training, love and affection, grooming, bathing, feeding, veterinary attention and nursing when they are sick or hurt.

Not only do you need time for all this, but you also need plenty of mental energy to pay attention to their needs throughout the day, as well as emotional energy to give them love and attention. Most of all, you have to be there with them. If you are out at work all day and lead a busy life during evening and weekends, a dog would not fit in. Once you have a dog, you can no longer go off for away days, long weekends and holidays at short notice without considering them.

Plenty of playing and training is necessary for dogs with active minds.

You will need to find someone reliable or a good kennel to look after them. You will need even more time for playing and exercising if you take on a dog that has lots of energy. Most dogs are active when young but some are more active than others.

Things to consider

Springer Spaniels have high energy levels and you will need plenty of time for play and exercise.

Male or female?

Individual dogs vary considerably, but some generalizations can be made. Usually, females are more placid, less competitive and more timid than males. Males are usually more boisterous, more confident and are slightly more prone to behaviour problems in later life. Male dogs cock their leg and females squat. This can be a consideration if you are a keen gardener. Both males and females make good pets in the right home. If you already have a dog, it is best to choose one of the opposite sex since a male and female are likely to get on better together than two dogs of the same sex.

Puppy or adult?

There are advantages and disadvantages to both. Puppies are very impressionable and you can mould them to suit your family's characters and lifestyle. Raising a puppy is a job for someone with lots of time on their hands as it is important to be with the puppy for most of its first year so that you can educate it properly.

If you have not got the time or you go out to work, consider getting an adult instead. Chewing and housetraining can take their toll on the furnishings and someone needs to be there most of the time to teach them right from wrong and to take them out to get used to the world.

If you had an old dog that has now passed on and you are thinking of getting a puppy, try hard to remember how much hard work they were. You may be 15 years older than you were last time and may not appreciate how much extra work is required to raise a puppy.

Adult dogs will have already formed their characters so it is important to choose wisely. They are usually past the housetraining and chewing phases, but expect them to take some time to settle into your home and routine. Adults may come ready trained and you have the satisfaction of knowing that you have rescued a dog with an uncertain future and given it a loving home.

Long or short tail?

Some breeds are 'traditionally docked', which means that part of the puppy's tail is cut off during the first few days of its life. This is done to suit a fashion and not for any purpose as dogs rarely injure intact tails even if they are working (breeders of docked breeds will often be adamant that they will damage their tails if left whole as a way to justify their actions). Whole tails are preferable as they enable the dog to signal its intentions and mood more easily. If you want a puppy from a docked breed with an intact tail, ask your breeder to reserve one for you and look elsewhere if they refuse.

In some countries, docking tails is illegal (Australia, Belgium, Finland, Germany, Iceland, Norway, Sweden, Switzerland) or can only be carried out by a veterinary surgeon for therapeutic reasons.

Pedigree or crossbred?

If you acquire a pedigree dog, you will know what size, shape, and temperament traits to expect, which is useful when buying a puppy. Mongrels are less predictable but, being a mixture, they tend not to have such strong traits as pedigrees and are often more suitable for pet purposes. Pedigree dogs are also subject to inherited diseases, whereas mongrels tend to be healthier.

Long or short coat?

The type of coat your dog has is important if it is to live in close proximity with you. A thick, profuse coat means that the dog is likely to shed continuously in a centrally heated house and may be uncomfortably hot in summer, leading to constant panting and bad temper. Daily brushing will be needed to remove loose hair, which will otherwise collect around the house. Fine, long coats need daily brushing to prevent mats from forming. Long-coated breeds have a covering of hair over their eyes, which can result in them being unable to see hands or people approaching making them more jumpy and nervous as a result unless it is tied back or cut off. Feathers (strands of hanging fur) on the legs and tail can carry mud and dirt.

If you have allergies, finding a dog with hair that grows continuously and does not shed may help. These dogs will need regular visits to the groomer to have the excess coat removed. Getting a dog with a coat that is easily maintained is important if you have neither the time nor inclination for lots of brushing.

What personality?

Before deciding on a breed or looking at puppies it is important to make a list of your requirements. Sit down as a family, or with a friend, and make a list of all the characteristics that would suit you, both psychological and physical, divided into essential and preferred.

Use the following chart to help. You may find the perfect breed, but you are more likely to have to compromise on certain traits and characteristics. In this case, make sure you do not compromise on essential traits, and pay particular attention to how you raise your puppy to ensure that traits you have compromised on do not cause a problem later.

Things to consider

Psychological characteristics

Personality

All breeds have their own unique blend of personality traits. Get to know the 'personality' of your chosen breeds and ask yourself if you would enjoy living with a dog with that character.

Strength of character

If you have a gentle nature, choose a dog to match, as strong characters need firm leadership.

Aloof/dependent

Some dogs like to form close emotional bonds with owners whereas others are happy to be more independent. If you like a close bond, chose a breed that likes to connect. If you prefer more distance, chose an aloof breed.

Biddable/willing to please

If you like a dog to enjoy doing as you ask, choose one that is biddable by nature. Some people prefer an independent character that wants to please himself and they should choose a dog that is not so keen to follow in their owner's footsteps.

Home alone

All dogs need to get used to being left gradually during puppyhood, but strong-natured, confident dogs usually cope better when alone than the nervous, reactive types.

Tactile and body contact

Some dogs like to be touched, stroked and cuddled, while others are not so keen. Finding a dog to match your desire for contact is important.

Psychological characteristics

Protectiveness

Confident dogs with strong characters are better at being protective in an adverse situation and less likely to back down. The downside of this is that they often have strong characters and are more likely to be aggressive if they need to make a point in other situations too. These dogs need careful control and socialization.

Watchdog

Some breeds are more reactive and alert than others and are easily encouraged to bark at the slightest disturbance. This can be useful or can be a nuisance depending on your point of view and your neighbours. Most dogs bark but it is easier to discourage a dog that was bred to be more relaxed.

Good with children

Dogs need to be socialized with children early in life if they are to like them. Some breeds tolerate children in the family but are not keen on visiting children, others get overwhelmed by too much noise and activity, some are so small they get injured easily by young children, and some are just right. Choosing a breed that is good with children is important if you have children in the family, are planning a family or if children visit on a regular basis.

Things to consider

Psychological characteristics

Good with other dogs

Dogs need to be socialized with others early in life if they are to get on well with them. Some breeds are known to be problematic with other dogs, particularly some of the terriers. If you have a lot of contact with other dogs, if you have another dog in the family, or if you want to be able to take your dog for walks where other dogs go, find a breed that will get on well with others.

Good with other pets

Predatory behaviour is common in certain breeds. Although dogs can be good under supervision with small pets they were raised with, it may be easier to get a dog with weaker instincts if you have small pets too. Cats and dogs can live well together once the dog has accepted the cat as part of its pack, but, again, it may be better to avoid terriers and dogs bred to chase and hunt, especially if you have a timid cat.

Good with strangers

Dogs need to be socialized well with people in early life if they are to get on well with them. Some dogs are more reactive and can be more aggressive as a result. If you have a sociable family, chose a dog that will be happy in the company of people.

Psychological characteristics

**Energy levels
and exercise requirements**

Some dogs have the energy and stamina to be active all day, whereas others are lazier. Choosing a dog to match your activity levels is essential if you do not want to live with a boisterous, under-exercised activity junky, or have to coax a reluctant layabout to go for long walks. Physical structure can have an effect on activity levels too as some dogs, such as those with squashed noses, very thick coats, or unusual-shaped bodies, may not be comfortable enough to be active.

**Busy, boisterous or
lazy in the house**

Dogs that are energetic out on a walk are not always busy or active in the house. Generally, smaller dogs are livelier indoors while larger dogs are content to lie around until there is something interesting to get up for. Some dogs will be into everything while others are content to observe from a distance.

**Height, weight and
physical strength**

Choosing the right size of dog is essential. Take into account the size of your house, car and garden or yard, as well as the people that it will be in contact with on a regular basis. Getting the right size of dog is particularly important if you have to consider small children or elderly or infirm relatives. When getting a second dog, consider the consequences if there is a large difference in their sizes and they fight or play roughly.

Things to consider

Health concerns

The disadvantage of breeding from selected dogs to create a 'pure' breed is an increase in the likelihood of puppies having inherited conditions that cause them health problems. Not all dogs will have the problems listed here, but enough dogs of this breed will have them to make it sensible for you to watch out for them. Before buying a pedigree puppy, always check to see if its parents have been screened for these conditions, and try to avoid buying puppies from lines where these problems have occurred. The following is a glossary of some of the more common health problems, most of which can be inherited. To find out more about these or any of the other health conditions listed, consult your veterinary surgeon.

Bloat – a life-threatening condition where the stomach swells up with gas or fluid. If the stomach twists it can develop into gastric torsion, which will require an immediate live-saving operation. It is most common in large dogs with deep, narrow chests, especially if they have a nervous or anxious temperament.

Cataracts – the lens of the eye becomes opaque leading to loss of functional vision. With problem breeds, this happens early in life rather than in old age as is more normal.

Congenital deafness – puppies with this condition are born deaf. It is most common in white, merle and piebald dogs.

Congenital heart disease – malformation of the heart and large blood vessels supplying the heart.

Ectropion – the eyelid is everted or rolled out, leading to increased exposure of the delicate membrane lining the eyelid. This can lead to infections, or damage due to drying out.

Elbow dysplasia – an inherited fault in the elbow joint that causes arthritis, pain and debilitation. Elbows of breeding dogs can and should be x-rayed to check for normality.

Entropion – an inward rolling of the eyelid edges leading to discomfort, pain, and scarring of the eye surface.

Epilepsy – an unpleasant condition where the dog has fits or seizures due to uncontrolled electrical activity in the brain.

Hip dysplasia – an inherited condition where the ball and socket joints of the hips do not fit well, leading to arthritis, pain and debilitation. Severe hip dysplasia can lead to the dog being unable to walk in later life. Dogs cannot be tested until they are two years of age, but hips of breeding dogs can and should be x-rayed and scored. A perfect score is 0:0 (one score for each hip). To be as sure as you can that your puppy will not get hip dysplasia, find a line where all your puppy's relatives have very low scores (less than 3).

Hypothyroidism – a disease of the thyroid which can be genetic in origin and usually appears in affected dogs between the ages of two and five years.

Legg-Calve-Perthes – a inherited disorder of the hip joint leading to stiffness and pain, commonly seen in puppies of miniature and toy breeds.

Osteochondritis dessicans – a disorder of the immature long bones, which can lead to cracks and damage at the joints causing pain and discomfort, particularly in the hind legs.

Patellar luxation – the kneecap on the hind leg pops out of position causing pain and lameness. It is an inherited condition and is common in very small or very large breeds. The physical symptoms may not be seen in puppies even if the deformity is present so all breeding stock should be checked for this condition.

Progressive retinal atrophy – an inherited disease that causes the retina of the eye to degenerate, leading to partial or total blindness. Age of onset varies, but once it begins, it is slow and progressive and cannot be cured.

Sebaceous adenitis – an inherited disease leading to inflammation of the sebaceous glands that causes excessive dandruff or scaling, hair loss, lesions, and a musty odour.

Von Willebrand's disease – a disorder where a vital clotting agent is missing in the dog's blood, leading to excessive bleeding on injury.

Gundogs

American Cocker Spaniel	Cataracts, progressive retinal atrophy, hip dysplasia, Legg-Calve-Perthes, luxating patellar, thyroid disorders, autoimmune conditions, skin problems, epilepsy, liver shunts, cherry eye
American Water Spaniel	Patellar luxation, progressive retinal atrophy, detached retina, cataracts, epilepsy, hypothyroidism, heart disease
Braque Italian	None known at present
Brittany	Hip dysplasia, glaucoma, spinal paralysis, seizures, heart and liver problems
Chesapeake Bay Retriever	Hip and elbow dysplasia, cataracts, osteochondritis dessicans, progressive retinal atrophy
Clumber Spaniel	Cataracts, entropion, spine problems, hip dysplasia
Cocker Spaniel (English)	Patellar luxation, progressive retinal atrophy, detached retina, cataracts, epilepsy, hypothyroidism, heart disease
Curly Coated Retriever	Hip dysplasia, progressive retinal atrophy, entropion, cataracts, bloat, hypothyroidism, epilepsy
English Setter	Hip and elbow dysplasia, cancer, hypothyroidism, deafness, eye disease and skin conditions

Health concerns

English Springer Spaniel	Hip dysplasia, progressive retinal atrophy and other eye conditions, epilepsy
Field Spaniel	Hip dysplasia, progressive retinal atrophy, hypothyroidism
Flat Coated Retriever	Prone to bone cancer, hip dysplasia, patellar luxation, progressive retinal atrophy, cataracts, entropion, hypothyroidism
German Shorthaired Pointer	Hip and elbow dysplasia, cataracts
German Wirehaired Pointer	Hip and elbow dysplasia, cataracts
Golden Retriever	Prone to obesity, skin conditions, eye problems, cataracts
Gordon Setter	Hip dysplasia, thyroid disease, progressive retinal atrophy, bloat, hypothyroidism
Hungarian Vizsla	Hip dysplasia, progressive retinal atrophy, entropion
Irish Red and White Setter	Hip dysplasia, cataracts and other eye problems, gastric torsion
Irish Setter	Hip dysplasia, progressive retinal atrophy, hypothyroidism, epilepsy, bloat
Irish Water Spaniel	Von Willebrand's disease, hip dysplasia, autoimmune diseases, epilepsy, hypothyroidism
Italian Spinone	Hip dysplasia, eye conditions, cerebella ataxia, bloat, ear infections
Kooikerhondje	Von Willebrand's disease, cataracts, patellar luxation, epilepsy, necrotizing myelopathy
Labrador Retriever	Prone to obesity, hip and elbow dysplasia, osteochondritis dessicans, cataracts, progressive retinal atrophy
Large Munsterlander	Hip dysplasia, cataracts, skin disorders
Nova Scotia Duck Tolling Retriever	Hip dysplasia, progressive retinal atrophy and other eye diseases, heart defects, hypothyroidism, Addison's disease, epilepsy, autoimmune disorders
Pointer	Hip and elbow dysplasia
Spanish Water Dog	None known at present
Sussex Spaniel	Eye problems, hip dysplasia, autoimmune diseases, heart defects, hypothyroidism
Weimaraner	Bloat, hip and elbow dysplasia
Welsh Springer Spaniel	Hip dysplasia, progressive retinal atrophy, cataracts, allergies, epilepsy, hypothyroidism and glaucoma
Wiredhaired Pointing Griffon	Hip dysplasia

Hounds

Afghan Hound	Hip dysplasia, cataracts, hypothyroidism, autoimmune disease
Basenji	Progressive retinal atrophy and other eye problems, malabsorption, anaemia, kidney problems
Basset Fauve de Bretagne	None known at present
Basset Griffon Vendeen (Petit and Grand)	Hip dysplasia, patellar luxation, eye problems, epilepsy, spine problems
Basset Hound	Osteochondritis dessicans, patellar luxation, elbow dysplasia, spinal problems, eye problems
Beagle	Eye problems, hypothyroidism, epilepsy, intervertebral disc disease
Black and Tan Coonhound	Hip dysplasia, eye problems
Bloodhound	Hip and elbow dysplasia, bloat, torsion, entropion, ectropion
Borzoi	Eye problems, bloat, heart disease, bone cancer, anaesthesia sensitivity
Dachshund (all types)	Spinal problems, elbow dysplasia, Legg-Calve-Perthes, patellar luxation, progressive retinal atrophy, cataracts, diabetes, epilepsy, painful spinal problems due to their long backs
Deerhound	Osteochondritis dessicans, bloat, cardiomyopathy, bone cancer, anaesthesia sensitivity
Elkhound	Hip dysplasia, progressive retinal atrophy, cataracts, kidney problems, hypothyroidism
Finnish Spitz	Cataracts
Foxhound (English and American)	None known at present
Grand Bleu de Gasgogne	Hip and elbow dysplasia, bloat
Greyhound	Progressive retinal atrophy, bloat, hypothyroidism, anaesthesia sensitivity
Hamiltonstövare	None known at present
Harrier	Hip dysplasia, eye disorders
Ibizan Hound	Axonal dystrophy, cardiomyopathy
Irish Wolfhound	Von Willebrand's disease, hip dysplasia, eye problems, bloat, bone cancer, cardiomyopathy
Lurcher	Bloat, anaesthesia sensitivity
Norwegian Lundehund	Intestinal lymphangiectasia, inflammatory bowel disease, enteropathy
Otterhound	Hip dysplasia, bloat, seizures
Pharaoh Hound	Mostly free of inherited diseases but sensitive to anaesthesia
Plott Hound	Bloat and gastric torsion

Rhodesian Ridgeback	Hip dysplasia, hypothyroidism, cancers, dermoid sinus
Saluki	Hip dysplasia, glaucoma, progressive retinal atrophy, hypothyroidism, heart defects
Segugio Italiano	Hip dysplasia, glaucoma, progressive retinal atrophy, hypothyroidism, heart defects
Sloughi	Hip dysplasia, cardiovascular problems, epilepsy, progressive retinal atrophy
Whippet	Eye conditions, sebaceous adenitis, heart defects

Pastoral

Anatolian Shepherd Dog	Hip and elbow dysplasia, entropion, hypothyroidism
Australian Cattle Dog	Eye defects, deafness
Australian Shepherd	Progressive retinal atrophy, eye conditions, epilepsy, deafness
Bearded Collie	Cataracts, Addison's disease, hypothyroidism, autoimmune disease
Belgian Shepherd Dog	
(Malinois)	Progressive retinal atrophy, pannus, cataracts, epilepsy, hypothyroidism
(Groenendael)	Progressive retinal atrophy, pannus, cataracts, epilepsy, hypothyroidism
(Laekenois)	Progressive retinal atrophy, pannus, cataracts, epilepsy, hypothyroidism
(Tervueren)	Elbow dysplasia, cataracts, epilepsy, hypothyroidism
Bergamasco	None known at present
Border Collie	Eye problems, progressive retinal atrophy, deafness, epilepsy
Briard	Progressive retinal atrophy, bloat, hypothyroidism
Collie (Rough)	Eye problems, deafness, hypothyroidism, heart problems
Collie (Smooth)	Eye problems, deafness, hypothyroidism, heart problems
Estrela Mountain Dog	Hip dysplasia
Finnish Lapphund	Progressive retinal atrophy
German Shepherd Dog (Alsatian)	Progressive retinal atrophy
Hungarian Kuvasz	Progressive retinal atrophy
Hungarian Puli	Progressive retinal atrophy, cataracts
Komondor	Hip dysplasia, bloat, entropion, cataracts
Lancashire Heeler	None known at present
Maremma Sheepdog	Hip dysplasia, bloat, anaesthesia sensitivity
Norwegian Buhund	Hip dysplasia, eye problems
Old English Sheepdog	Eye disorders, cataracts, diabetes, deafness, hypothyroidism, Wobbler's syndrome

Polish Lowland Sheepdog	Heart defects
Pyrenean Mountain Dog	Hip and elbow dysplasia, patellar luxation, cataracts, entropion, bleeding disorders, spinal problems, anaesthesia sensitivity
Pyrenean Sheepdog	None known at present
Samoyed	Hip dysplasia, progressive retinal atrophy, cataracts, hypothyroidism, sebaceous adenitis, diabetes
Shetland Sheepdog	Digestive disorders, eye conditions, hypothyroidism, epilepsy, prone to leg bone fractures, Legg-Calve-Perthes
Swedish Vallhund	Some eye conditions including progressive retinal atrophy
Welsh Corgi (Cardigan and Pembroke)	Eye disorders, spine problems

Terriers

Airedale Terrier	Hypothyroidism, bleeding disorders
American Staffordshire Terrier	Cataracts, hypothyroidism, cruciate ligament ruptures, cancers
Australian Terrier	Hip problems, patellar luxation, diabetes, Legg-Calve-Perthes
Bedlington Terrier	Cataracts, patellar luxation
Border Terrier	Patellar luxation, cataracts, autoimmune problems, hypothyroidism, heart problems, Legg-Calve-Perthes
Bull Terrier (English)	Patellar luxation, eye problems, heart defects, deafness, kidney problems, skin inflammation
Bull Terrier (Miniature)	Patellar luxation, eye problems, heart defects, deafness, kidney problems, skin inflammation
Cairn Terrier	Hip problems, patellar luxation, progressive retinal atrophy, blood disorders, kidney problems, Legg-Calve-Perthes
Cesky Terrier	Ovarian cysts, painful spinal problems due to their long back, eye problems
Dandie Dinmont Terrier	Glaucoma, Cushings, thyroid, painful spinal problems due to their long back
Fox Terrier (Smooth)	Eye and heart defects, epilepsy, Legg-Calve-Perthes
Fox Terrier (Wire)	Eye and heart defects, epilepsy
Glen of Imaal Terrier	Hip dysplasia, progressive retinal atrophy, skin allergies
Irish Terrier	Hyperthyroidism, cataracts
Jack Russell Terrier	None known at present

Kerry Blue Terrier	Cataracts, blood disorders
Lakeland Terrier	Hip and elbow dysplasia, cataracts, Legg-Calve-Perthes
Manchester Terrier	Hip dysplasia, Legg-Calve-Perthes, progressive retinal atrophy, seizures, hypothyroidism, limbs break easily when young
Norfolk Terrier	Patellar luxation, heart defects, epilepsy
Norwich Terrier	Patellar luxation, heart defects, epilepsy
Parson Russell Terrier	Hip problems, patellar luxation, eye problems
Scottish Terrier	Hypothyroidism, lymphoma, Legg-Calve-Perthes
Sealyham Terrier	Eye problems, spinal problems, heart defects, deafness
Skye Terrier	Elbow dysplasia, bone growth problems, hypothyroidism, painful spinal problems due to long back
Soft Coated Wheaten Terrier	Progressive retinal atrophy, cataracts, kidney disease
Welsh Terrier	Patellar luxation, eye conditions, Legg-Calve-Perthes
West Highland White Terrier	Skin conditions, hip problems, Legg-Calve-Perthes, cataracts

Toys

Affenpinscher	Luxating patellar, hip problems, Legg-Calve-Perthes, open fontanels, thyroid problems, heart defects, eye problems, leg breaks while a puppy
Australian Silken Terrier	Patellar luxation, Legg-Calve-Perthes, hypoglycaemia, liver shunts
Bichon Frise	Patellar luxation, Legg-Calve-Perthes, progressive retinal atrophy, cataracts, epilepsy, gum disease
Bolognese	Luxating patellar, eye conditions
Cavalier King Charles Spaniel	Heart defects, patellar luxation, cataracts, retinal problems
Chihuahua (Longhaired or Smooth coated)	Patellar luxation, Legg-Calve-Perthes, eye defect, heart conditions, hypoglycaemia, tracheal collapse
Chinese Crested	Patellar luxation, several different eye conditions, closed ear canals and epilepsy
English Toy Terrier (Black and Tan, Toy Manchester Terrier)	Hip problems, progressive retinal atrophy, hypothyroidism, seizures, limbs break easily when young
Griffon Bruxellois	Patellar luxation, progressive retinal atrophy
Havanese	Patellar luxation, cataracts, hypothyroidism

Italian Greyhound	Patellar luxation, progressive retinal atrophy, autoimmune disease
Japanese Chin	Patellar luxation, progressive retinal atrophy, cataracts, seizures, anaesthesia sensitivity
King Charles Spaniel	Patellar luxation, cataracts, inguinal hernias, heart problems, anaesthesia sensitivity
Lowchen	Patellar luxation, progressive retinal atrophy, cataracts
Maltese	Patellar luxation, progressive retinal atrophy, entropion, glaucoma, hypothyroidism, hypoglycaemia, deafness, dental problems
Miniature Pinscher	Patellar luxation, hip problems, Legg-Calve-Perthes, progressive retinal atrophy, cataracts, pannus
Papillon	Patellar luxation, eye problems, teeth problems
Pekingese	Pastern and patellar luxation, Legg-Calve-Perthes, dry eye, spinal problems,
Pomeranian	Patellar luxation, Legg-Calve-Perthes, progressive retinal atrophy, cataracts, entropion, hypoglycaemia, tracheal collapse, dental problems
Pug	Hip problems, Legg-Calve-Perthes, progressive retinal atrophy, cataracts, entropion, dry eye, epilepsy, liver disease, anaesthesia sensitivity
Toy Fox Terrier (American Toy Terrier)	Patellar luxation, demodectic mange, hip problems, bleeding disorcers, hypothyroidism
Yorkshire Terrier	Patellar luxation, Legg-Calve-Perthes, hypoglycaemia, liver shunts, dental problems, collapsed trachea

Utility Dogs

Akita	Hip dysplasia, patellar luxation, progressive retinal atrophy, bloat, bleeding disorders, hypothyroidism, sebaceous adenitis, pemphigus, lupus, cancer
American Eskimo Dog	Patellar luxation, progressive retinal atrophy, diabetes
Boston Terrier	Patellar luxation, Legg-Calve-Perthes, cataracts, epilepsy, heart problems, deafness
Bulldog	Cataracts, ectropion, entropion, dry eye, elongated soft palate, heart defects, hypothyroidism, hip dysplasia, small trachea
Canaan Dog	Hip dysplasia, hypothyroidism, eye problems
Chow Chow	Hip dysplasia, patellar luxation, growth disorders of the joints, entropion, glaucoma, stenotic nares, hypothyroidism, kidney problems, some skin and hormone problems
Dalmation	Progressive retinal atrophy, glaucoma, diabetes, deafness, bladder stones
French Bulldog	Elbow dysplasia, patellar luxation, cataracts, entropion, elongated soft pulate, spinal problems, stenotic nares
German Spitz (Klein)	Patellar luxation, progressive retinal atrophy, epilepsy, dental problems

German Spitz (Mittel)   Patellar luxation, progressive retinal atrophy, epilepsy, dental problems

Japanese Shiba Inu   Patellar luxation, hypothyroidism

Japanese Spitz   Patella luxation

Keeshond   Patellar luxation, eye problems, hypothyroidism, epilepsy

Lhasa Apso   Patellar luxation, progressive retinal atrophy, entropion, bleeding disorders, spinal problems

Miniature Schnauzer   Juvenile cataracts, progressive retinal atrophy, Legg-Calve-Perthes, epilepsy, pancreatitis, hypothyroidism, bleeding disorders, liver disorders, dental problems

Schnauzer (Standard)   Hip dysplasia, hypothyroidism, cataracts, cancer

Poodle (Miniature)   Hip problems, Legg-Calve-Perthes, patellar luxation, progressive retinal atrophy, cataracts, glaucoma, deafness, heart defects, epilepsy (recommended for first time owners, especially if they are prone to allergies – care is needed to find a healthy dog free of inherited disease)

Poodle (Standard)   Eye defects, cataracts, Legg-Calve-Perthes, entropion, epilepsy, bloat, sebaceous adenitis

Poodle (Toy)   Patellar luxation, Legg-Calve-Perthes, cataracts, progressive retinal atrophy, epilepsy, hypoglycaemia

Schipperke   Hip problems, Legg-Calve-Perthes, progressive retinal atrophy, cataracts, entropion, hypothyroidism, epilepsy

Shar Pei   Demodectic mange, amyloidosis, hypothyroidism, bloat, malabsorption, autoimmune diseases, kidney problems, skin disease and entropion (find a healthy line who's dogs have not had to have their eyelids surgically altered)

Shih Tzu   Kidney problems, blood disorders

Tibetan Spaniel   Progressive retinal atrophy, patella luxation

Tibetan Terrier   Patellar luxation, progressive retinal atrophy, lens luxation, cataracts, hypothyroidism, bleeding disorders

Working Dogs

Alaskan Malamute   Hip dysplasia, bloat, kidney problems, hypothyroidism, progressive retinal atrophy, bleeding disorders

Beauceron   Bloat

Bernese Mountain Dog   Hip dysplasia, elbow dysplasia, osteochondritis dessicans, progressive retinal atrophy, thyroid problems, tumours, bloat, kidney disease

Greater Swiss   Hip, elbow or shoulder dysplasia, osteochondritis dessicans, bloat, torsion,

Mountain Dog	hypothyroidism, splenic torsion, dilated oesophagus
Bouvier Des Flandres	Hip dysplasia, cataracts, glaucoma, entropion, torsion, hypothyroidism, laryngeal paralysis, cancer
Boxer	Hip dysplasia, progressive retinal atrophy, heart problems, torsion, epilepsy, bleeding disorders, cancers, intestinal problems
Bullmastiff	Hip and elbow dysplasia, eye problems, bloat and torsion, heart defects
Dobermann	Hip dysplasia, bloat, cancers, von Willebrand's disease, liver disease, hypothyroidism, heart defects
Giant Schnauzer	Hip dysplasia, osteochondritis dessicans, progressive retinal atrophy, glaucoma, heart defects, epilepsy
Great Dane	Hip and elbow dysplasia, cataracts, bone cancer, bloat
Greenland Dog	None known at present
Hovawart	Hip dysplasia, thyroid problems
Leonberger	Hip dysplasia, bloat, cancer, hypothyroidism, osteochondritis dessicans, Addison's disease, and cardiomyopathy
Mastiff	Hip and elbow dysplasia, joint and bone problems, eye defects, hypothyroidism, heart defects, bloat, epilepsy
Neapolitan Mastiff	Hip and elbow dysplasia, joint and bone problems, hypothyroidism, heart defects, entropion, bloat
Newfoundland	Hip dysplasia, osteochondritis dessicans, bloat, heart problems, eyelid problems, hypothyroidism
Pinscher (German)	Hip dysplasia, eye problems
Portuguese Water Dog	Hip dysplasia, progressive retinal atrophy
Rottweiler	Hip and elbow dysplasia, osteochondritis dessicans, eye defects, heart defects, cancer, bloat, hypothyroidism
Russian Black Terrier	Hip and elbow dysplasia, eye problems
Siberian Husky	Hip dysplasia, eye defects, progressive retinal atrophy
St Bernard	Hip dysplasia, osteochondritis dessicans, bloat, cancer, epilepsy, entropion, ectropion, heart problems
Tibetan Mastiff	Hip dysplasia, hypothyroidism

Health concerns

Choosing a breeder

It is worth taking the time to find a good breeder. Conscientious breeders take care when producing their stock and the puppies they produce are likely to be healthier and have better temperaments. Unfortunately, pedigree puppies fetch a high price and there are many unscrupulous breeders who churn out many litters of poor-quality puppies to make a quick profit.

Where to buy a puppy

Avoid places that keep many different breeds of puppy under the same roof. It is very likely that these puppies came from puppy farms and you may end up with problems as a result. It is also very easy to buy on impulse from such places without giving the purchase proper consideration.

Sources to avoid

Avoid breeders who breed a number of different breeds, have many different puppies available, and keep them and their mothers outside in kennels. The 'professional' breeder may have lots of knowledge about their breeds, but with so many dogs to care for it is less likely they will make the same effort to raise and socialize each puppy as would a breeder who specializes in one breed and breeds only one litter at a time and raises them in their house.

Avoid buying a puppy from an advert in the paper or from a pet shop. Both of these can be outlets for puppy farmers who keep dogs in small cages, breed from them continuously, and often take the puppies away from the mother too early. The resulting puppies are often physically compromised, unhealthy and may show abnormal behaviour caused by the early stress. It is not possible to tell whether a puppy comes from such a place just by its appearance so it is better to avoid these outlets altogether.

Puppy farmers go to some lengths to disguise their trade. They may arrange to meet you in a car park or service station close to your home. Once there, it is very difficult to say no when you see the puppy, even if, or perhaps especially if it is not well. Or they may deliver the puppy to a colleague's home so that you see the puppies there rather than on their premises. The mother will not be with them and the puppies have often travelled a long distance. A favourite trick is to breed from larger parents so that the resulting puppies are larger than usual. They can then be sold earlier, often being taken away from their mother too soon.

Registration

Most pedigree puppies are registered with the national Kennel Club and the registration papers are given to you when you buy a puppy to show their parentage. It is important to know that Kennel Club registration is not an indication of quality or a seal of approval. Anyone, including irresponsible or unscrupulous breeders, can register their litter with their national Kennel Club. Sadly, at present, there is no large organization that

monitors breeders and provides information on quality of the puppies they breed. Therefore it is up to the individual to be as informed as possible and to choose their breeder carefully using the information in this chapter.

Motivation for breeders

In our modern world, very few dogs work for their living. There are some exceptions, such as police dogs, sniffer dogs, dogs for disabled people, gundogs and sheepdogs, but the majority of dogs in Western countries are now kept as pets.

Most pedigree pet dogs are bred by breeders who are aiming to further their breed. They sell excess puppies, keeping the best to show and breed from.

Puppies should be healthy, free from genetic diseases, well socialized and habituated, and have sound temperaments.

Choosing a breeder

Motivations vary, but dog shows reward breeders who can produce a dog that comes closest to the breed standard. The breed standard is a list of physical characteristics such as position of ears, or length of tail. Hence the dog is judged on and awarded prizes for how it looks rather than on how it behaves.

Unscrupulous breeders

The show system allows unscrupulous breeders to get away with paying no attention to temperament as long as they can get their dog to behave while being shown. Many show dogs live their lives in kennels and are handled only by skilled handlers. Consequently, adverse behavioural traits can be masked and unless the breeder takes care to monitor the progress of their progeny, they may not be aware, or care, that they are selling potentially difficult dogs to pet owners.

Since prizes are not awarded for temperament, unscrupulous breeders can get away with selling stock with less than perfect temperament. When seeing a litter of puppies, it is impossible to tell whether they have good natures or not. Once their true nature has been revealed, most people are too attached to their puppies to take them back. Since an adult dog's character is influenced by both genetics and upbringing, unscrupulous breeders can blame bad upbringing instead of accepting that bad breeding may be the cause.

Signs of a good breeder

Fortunately, there are many responsible breeders who care very much about the temperament of the dogs they are breeding and what happens to them in the future. These breeders will take the utmost care to place their puppies in responsible homes and will usually closely question potential buyers to ensure they are going to good homes. They breed for temperament as well as physical conformation, taking care to choose good-natured parents. They stay in touch with owners of their puppies and help with problems and re-homing if necessary. Finding a good breeder is not easy but is essential if you want a well-adjusted puppy.

Many puppies are bred so the breeder can keep the pick of the litter with the hope that it will become a winner in the show ring.

Good breeders take care to select good parents, provide proper health care, take time to raise a litter properly and put in a lot of effort to ensure well-adjusted, healthy puppies. They rarely breed more than two or three litters a year, sometimes less than that.

Finding a good breeder is definitely worth the effort. You may like to begin by going to dog shows and talking to breeders and owners there about their dogs. Dog shows are advertised in the specialist dog press or via the internet. Find out about breed clubs and ask people who run them how to find a good breeder. Usually, these people are real breed enthusiasts and will have lots of useful knowledge. Ask people who own nice dogs of your chosen breed where their dog came from and talk to their breeder.

Good breeders do not breed often and do not breed to order. They will be able to tell you when their next litter is planned so be prepared to wait – if you have chosen your breeder well, it will be worth it.

A good breeder is one who fulfills the following criteria. Be prepared to ask questions and if you cannot get satisfactory answers, look elsewhere.

Mongrels and crossbreds

As well as pedigree puppies, mongrel or crossbred puppies are often available from friends or rescue societies. Guessing what their adult size and inherited traits will be like is difficult, but they can make very good pets if you do not mind taking a chance.

Mongrels and crossbreds come in all shapes, sizes, colours, coat types and temperaments. Each one is unique. Crossbreds are mixes of two or more pedigrees while mongrels are a mixture of all breeds. They usually live for 12–16 years. Their exercise needs vary widely and they are often less prone to inherited disorders than purebreds.

Puppies may be tired when you visit if they have just been playing and feeding, but they will soon wake up and begin to show their developing personalities.

Happy and healthy puppies

The breeder should be able to tell you all the inherited medical conditions that are prevalent in the breed (find out what these are before you talk to breeders). They should have had the necessary genetic tests done on the breeding stock they have used for breeding and be able to provide the relevant certificates.

They should be willing to talk about inherited medical conditions present in their lines as well as the faults that their own dog may have. A good breeder will offer a health guarantee as well as a guarantee that they will refund your money if it turns out that the puppy they have sold you has a genetically inherited condition. The breeder will have selected parents with good temperaments. Ask them why they chose these particular parents to produce the litter and how they knew about the temperament of the father. It may also be a good idea to ask about the temperament of previous puppies they have bred, particularly if they have used the same parents before. Ask if they are willing to allow you to contact owners of previous puppies for a recommendation or perhaps see letters or photographs from satisfied customers.

The mother is with the puppies

Meeting the mother of the puppies is very important. Half of the genetic make-up of your future dog is due to her and it is important that you like what you see. Gently insist on seeing the mother and be suspicious if your request is refused.

Puppies that are raised with plenty of human contact will be bold and outgoing with strangers and will approach readily.

The mother of the puppies should be well adjusted with people and readily accept the arrival of visitors. Maternal hormones heighten any behaviour problems a bitch may have, including nervous aggression towards strangers. If the breeder says she is only like it when she has puppies, that may be true, but she still has an underlying problem whether it is usually displayed or not. If you have to meet the mother in different room to the puppies, look elsewhere. If she is in the next cage barking and growling at you, the puppies will see and smell her fear and may show the same behaviour to strangers when they are older. If the bitch is not on the premises, ask why. If you are told she is out for a walk, wait until she returns or come back later to meet her. The breeder should also be able to show you pictures of and provide information about the puppies' father. Contact his owner and ask about his temperament. Better still, arrange to go and see him for yourself.

The puppies live in the house

The best place for pet puppies to be raised is in a house. There they can experience and get used to all the noises, smells, and sights that accompany life in close proximity to humans. They get used to walking on carpets, playing with children, hearing pots and pans crashing, going up and down steps, and a host of other thing that will get them ready for life as a pet.

Puppies make messes, and a litter of puppies make a lot of mess, so do not expect to find them in the living room. However, they should not be so far away from the house that they are unlikely to spend any time there or only be taken in for occasional visits. If necessary, ask to see what the puppies are like in the house. If they slink about looking worried, then that is how they will behave in your house and in anywhere else new. A well-adjusted puppy will walk in confidently, investigating every corner.

Motherhood can be a stressful time for bitches and any underlying behaviour problem may come to the surface.

Good health

The puppies you see should be bouncing with health and vigour with shiny coats and a zest for life. If you want to be completely sure, or if you have any doubts, ask for a check to be made by a veterinary surgeon before you take the puppy home (be prepared to pay for this). A good breeder will be happy to allow this.

The place where the puppies are kept should be clean and sweet-smelling. There should be separate, obvious places for sleeping and toileting with all puppies being able to move easily from one place to the other. Puppies kept in places where all of the pen is covered with the same substrate (usually straw or shredded paper) can be very hard to housetrain as they have not practised the instinctive action of moving away from their nest to relieve themselves.

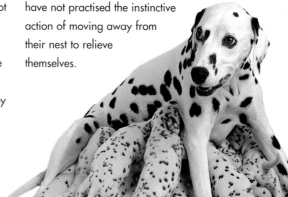

Choosing a breeder

Are you a suitable owner?

Be prepared to be questioned by a caring breeder as they want to know that you will make a good owner. If they do not seem to care about you and how you will treat the puppy they will sell you, they may not care about anything other than making money.

The puppies are being socialized

Puppies need to get used to people, other dogs and other animals while still in the litter if they are to be friendly and unafraid later in life. A great deal of effort is needed to ensure that a litter of puppies meets a gradually increasing number of new faces, young and old. Puppies should have met and played with men and women, toddlers, school-age children and teenagers before they go to their new homes. Take someone of the opposite sex with you to check their response to both men and women. Many puppies are raised by women and may never see a man until they go to new homes, with the result that they are anxious and worried by them. If the puppies are shy and keep away from you, it is likely they have not had sufficient contact with strangers. Look elsewhere for a breeder who takes more care with socialization.

As well as getting used to people and other animals, it is important for young puppies to get used sounds, smells and sights that they will see later in life. If this is done early, the puppy will be unafraid and well adjusted. This happens naturally if puppies are kept in

Puppies raised in a house will be more able to cope with life as a pet than those raised in a kennel.

a busy household, but special effort is needed if puppies spend a lot of time in a quiet pen. Check to see if breeders make an effort to get their puppies used to vacuum cleaners, washing machines, different surfaces, different smells and other sights and sounds that humans take for granted. Puppies should also have been out in the car and have got used to being alone without their mother or littermates before they leave the litter. Although puppies have new immune systems and need protection from diseases, they should also have had meetings with vaccinated adult dogs, other than their own breed. If puppies are born in a busy household, most of this happens naturally. If the household is quiet, a good breeder will have made an extra effort to ensure adequate socialization.

Ask the breeder what they have done to ensure the puppies are well socialized. A good breeder will know how to socialize puppies well and will be able to make recommendations for you to continue the process.

The breeder knows their stuff

Good breeders are knowledgeable about their breed and about dogs in general. They will not need to impress you, but you should be impressed by how much they know. Breeders who have been breeding for years may not always be knowledgeable, and people who claim to know 'everything about dogs' probably do not.

Aftercare is on offer

A good breeder will offer advice during the life of your dog (providing you call them for serious matters rather for trivial issues) or be able to refer you to someone who can help. They will be interested in your puppy's progress and may ask you to let them know each year how it is getting on, perhaps inviting you back for annual reunions with other puppy owners. They should also be prepared to take back the dog at any time if you cannot keep it or at least help you find an alternative home.

Take your time to get to know your chosen puppy and decide whether he has the right personality for you and your family.

A good breeder will

- Be concerned about the health and temperament of the puppies.
- Allow you to see the mother with the puppies.
- Let the puppies live in the house or have regular access.
- Socialize the puppies with people and other animals and get them used to things they will encounter when older.
- Be knowledgeable about dogs.
- Care about what happens to the puppies.

Choosing a breeder

Finding an adult dog

The advantages of acquiring an adult dog are obvious – what you see is what you get as their body shape, size and character are already formed and they are usually past the chewing and housetraining stages.

Although someone else has raised them and moulded them to their way of life, dogs are adaptable and readily accept new ways of doing things if you have the patience to teach them. Older dogs are slightly more set in their ways but the older the dog, the more likely it is that it has been a successful pet in the past.

Places to find adult dogs

There are a number of places where you can find adult dogs for either sale or adoption. It is best to explore all places that re-home dogs in your area as the quality of the information about the dogs held there, and hence your ability to choose the right dog for you, will depend upon the people responsible for looking after that particular dog. As in all walks of life, there are good and bad establishments and it is best to shop around until you find an appropriate source for a dog.

Be prepared to take your time looking for the right dog for you and perhaps visit several places several times. If you have a young family, it may be best to go without the children at first so that you can find a dog with a suitable nature rather than have the children insist on one that looks cute. If there is nothing suitable, look elsewhere. Do not be emotionally blackmailed into

Many adult dogs are looking for good homes and they can make perfect pets for loving families.

taking a dog as 'otherwise he will be put to sleep'. There are thousands of dogs out there looking for homes (and sadly thousands of unwanted dogs being put to sleep everyday) and it is better that you find the right dog for your family than take on one that will make both of you unhappy just because you wanted to save him or her.

Rescue centres

Rescue shelters range from the national networks of homes run by large charities to small backyard concerns. The quality and professionalism of these centres depends on who runs them and it is best to ask friends and other animal professionals to get recommendations of the best in your area.

Rescue centres are expensive to run. The dogs are cared for, vaccinated, given health checks, properly fed, neutered and retrained if necessary. All this costs money so do expect to pay a reasonably high donation to the charity based on the market prices for such procedures.

Modern rescue centres should be light, airy places where the dogs are well cared for, given as much attention as possible and are happy. However, some are not and the dogs may look like they are in prison. Be prepared to harden your heart and go armed with your list of 'essential and preferred characteristics'. Try hard not to fall in love with any dog before you have made a sensible decision about whether or not it would suit your family's requirements. Above all, take advice from the rescue centre staff. It is in everyone's interests for you to get a suitable pet rather than rush a decision.

Due to the pressures of life in a kennel, a dog will not behave in the same way as that dog would at home. You will see a slightly distorted view of its behaviour and it is important to ask the staff that look after him what he is really like.

Assessing dogs in kennels is not easy and it is important to ask advice from the staff who will know the dog's personalitiy.

Finding an adult dog

Finding an adult dog

The right adult dog for you can bring you years of happiness and love.

Try to get opinions from several different staff and take the dog out to a quiet place to get to know him. Play with him, stroke him, groom him and see what he is like with other dogs, strangers and children. It is not easy to decide on a new dog in just one or two meetings, and if you are new to dog ownership, take a friend who has more experience with you to help. If the rescue centre will let you reserve your chosen dog, try to go back every day for a few days to visit him and get to know him better so that you are sure before you make the final decision.

Breed rescues

Breed rescues are organizations that re-home dogs of a particular breed. If you are interested in one breed but require an adult rather than a puppy, find out from the Kennel Club about your local breed rescue. Breed rescues rarely have kennels and the dogs are fostered by caring owners of the breed. This gives you a lot of information about that particular dog as the foster carers will have lived with that dog and will know what it is like. The disadvantage is that you may not have many dogs to chose from so be prepared to wait or travel further afield if they do not have a dog to meet your requirements. You may feel under a lot of pressure to take a dog they are offering, so be prepared to resist until you have had time to consider and weigh up the pros and cons of taking on that particular dog.

Breeders

Breeders sometimes keep several puppies into adulthood to see which will be best for showing. If these dogs have lived all their life in kennels, they will not be good pet dogs. Similarly, breeders sometimes decide to 'retire' their brood bitches into pet homes. These dogs may not have lived in a house, may not be accustomed to life with people and may not have met many other people or unfamiliar dogs. They have usually lived mostly with other dogs and so are very dog-oriented. They make very poor pets and are nervous and difficult to rehabilitate. Be prepared for a long haul if you get such a dog but, if possible, avoid them altogether unless you know the dog was kept as a pet. Sometimes caring breeders (see previous chapter) will have taken back a dog they have bred when the owner could no longer keep it. If the dog has been raised well by the previous owner and has a good temperament, this may make a very suitable pet for you. Visit and take time to get to know the dog, and be prepared to say no if you do not like what you see.

Friends

A good place to get a dog is through a friend who, for a good reason, can no longer keep their dog. If you already know the dog well and like it, there will be no surprises. Do not take on a dog as a favour to your friend. If the dog does not suit you, you may both be unhappy and ultimately, you may fall out with your friend anyway. Someone you know may know of someone who has a dog they want to give up. Again, go and visit but be prepared to say no politely and walk away if it is not suitable for you.

Advertisements

This is probably the worst way to find an adult dog. Finding a good dog via an advert is a bit of a lottery. You may be lucky, but you may not. Question the owners at length before you go. If they do not have the answers, they may not be the original owner and it will be very difficult for you to decide just by looking at the dog if he is the right one for you. If they are a bit cagey about the answers, they may not be telling you the truth so beware. If you have to travel to see the dog, your family will already have expectations and will have given the dog all sorts of fanciful qualities before you even get there.

Saying no is difficult, especially if the dog does not have a very good home. If you must find a dog via an advertisement, spend some time with the dog once you are there so that you get to know it well, and perhaps even ask to take it for a walk. Go with the intention of going back for another visit so that you have time to consider properly. Do not be swayed by the owner saying that there is someone coming to see the dog later so he may be gone when you come back later.

How to use this guide

The descriptions of the breeds given here are broad generalizations based on a range of opinions from people who know the breed well. There will be some dogs that don't fit the description, but, in general, these personality traits will be seen in most dogs of this breed.

How to use this guide

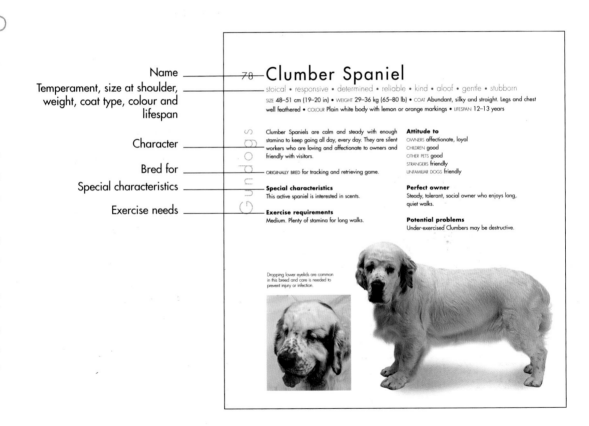

Name

Temperament, size at shoulder, weight, coat type, colour and lifespan

Character

Bred for

Special characteristics

Exercise needs

78 Clumber Spaniel

stoical • responsive • determined • reliable • kind • aloof • gentle • stubborn

SIZE 48–51 cm (19–20 in) • WEIGHT 29–36 kg (65–80 lb) • COAT Abundant, silky and straight. Legs and chest well feathered • COLOUR Plain white body with lemon or orange markings • LIFESPAN 12–13 years

Gundogs

Clumber Spaniels are calm and steady with enough stamina to keep going all day, every day. They are silent workers who are loving and affectionate to owners and friendly with visitors.

ORIGINALLY BRED for tracking and retrieving game.

Special characteristics
This active spaniel is interested in scents.

Exercise requirements
Medium. Plenty of stamina for long walks.

Attitude to
OWNERS affectionate, loyal
CHILDREN good
OTHER PETS good
STRANGERS friendly
UNFAMILIAR DOGS friendly

Perfect owner
Steady, tolerant, social owner who enjoys long, quiet walks.

Potential problems
Under-exercised Clumbers may be destructive.

Dropping lower eyelids are common in this breed and care is needed to prevent injury or infection.

Whether the breed is good with children, other pets, strangers and unfamiliar dogs is, again, based on the knowledge of many individuals. Much will depend on its upbringing and socialization, so the information given here is for an average dog and owner.

Behaviour problems listed here are based on experience of dogs of this breed that go wrong. Not all dogs of this particular breed will have these behaviour problems, but some dogs of this breed will exhibit them or will have these tendencies.

The description of the perfect owner is given so that you can match your own characteristics against them. If you do not match the description, consider how this will affect a dog of this breed if it came to live with you and your family and look again at the other breeds for one that is more suitable.

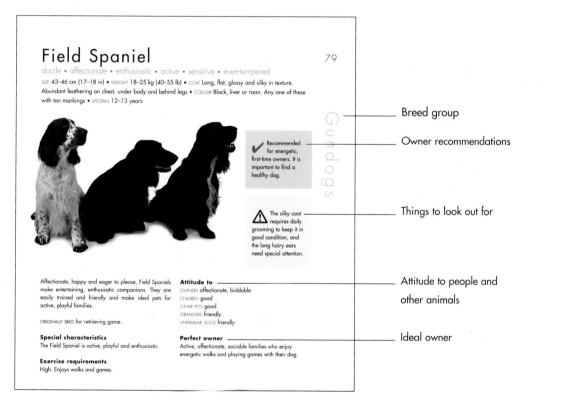

Field Spaniel

79

docile • affectionate • enthusiastic • active • sensitive • even-tempered

SIZE 43–46 cm (17–18 in) • WEIGHT 18–25 kg (40–55 lb) • COAT Long, flat, glossy and silky in texture. Abundant feathering on chest, under body and behind legs • COLOUR Black, liver or roan. Any one of these with tan markings • LIFESPAN 12–13 years

✔ Recommended for energetic, first-time owners. It is important to find a healthy dog.

⚠ The silky coat requires daily grooming to keep it in good condition, and the long hairy ears need special attention.

Affectionate, happy and eager to please, Field Spaniels make entertaining, enthusiastic companions. They are easily trained and friendly and make ideal pets for active, playful families.

ORIGINALLY BRED for retrieving game.

Special characteristics
The Field Spaniel is active, playful and enthusiastic.

Exercise requirements
High. Enjoys walks and games.

Attitude to
OWNERS affectionate, biddable
CHILDREN good
OTHER PETS good
STRANGERS friendly
UNFAMILIAR DOGS friendly

Perfect owner
Active, affectionate, sociable families who enjoy energetic walks and playing games with their dog.

Breed group

Owner recommendations

Things to look out for

Attitude to people and other animals

Ideal owner

How to use this guide

Gundogs

Braque Italian (Bracco)

sensible • slightly stubborn • sensitive • gentle • even-tempered

SIZE **55–67 cm (22–26½ in)** • WEIGHT **25–40 kg (55–88 lb)** • COAT **Short, dense** • COLOUR **White.**
White with orange, amber or chestnut markings. White may be speckled. Roan with solid markings
• LIFESPAN **12–13 years**

Gundogs

These dogs have the energy and enthusiasm to hunt all day and be ready to get up the next day and do it all again. Gentle and placid at home, they are tolerant, slightly stubborn but playful companions.

ORIGINALLY BRED for tracking, pointing, and retrieving on land and in water.

Special characteristics
A vigorous hunter, the Braque Italian is energetic and playful.

Exercise requirements
High. Quiet at home, but it needs plenty of long walks and free running.

Attitude to
OWNERS **placid**
CHILDREN **tolerant**
OTHER PETS **may be problematic with smaller pets**
STRANGERS **usually friendly**
UNFAMILIAR DOGS **usually friendly**

Perfect owner
Active families who enjoy long energetic walks, require a calm, gentle-natured pet at home and who do not desire enthusiastic responses to obedience requests.

Potential problems
This dog's enthusiasm may lead to control problems on walks.

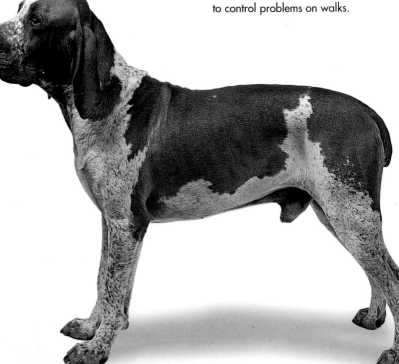

Brittany

energetic • responsive • busy • affectionate • enthusiastic

SIZE 46–52 cm (18½–20 in) • WEIGHT 13–15 kg (28–33 lb) • COAT Dense, fairly fine and slightly wavy • COLOUR Orange/white, liver/white, black/white, tricolour, or roan of any of these colours • LIFESPAN 13–15 years

Enthusiastic, responsive Brittanys are energetic, reactive workaholics that are happiest when busy. Not a dog to leave behind at home while you work and party, these active dogs need both company and a job to do.

ORIGINALLY BRED for setting and flushing game, as well as pointing and retrieving.

Special characteristics
Playful, busy and active, the Brittany revels in exercise.

Exercise requirements
High. Busy in the house and energetic outside.

Attitude to
OWNERS willing to please
CHILDREN good-natured, playful
OTHER PETS good
STRANGERS usually friendly
UNFAMILIAR DOGS usually friendly

Perfect owner
Active, busy owner who loves to play with their dog and include it in all aspects of life.

Potential problems
Some lines of these dogs may be aggressive to strangers.

Gundogs

Hungarian Vizsla

lively • responsive • obedient • sensitive • affectionate • biddable

SIZE **53–64 cm (21–25 in)** • WEIGHT **20–30 kg (44–66 lb)** • COAT **Short, dense. Also less common wire-haired variety** • COLOUR **Russet gold** • LIFESPAN **13–14 years**

Gundogs

Sensitive, energetic Vizslas have plenty of energy and exuberance, especially when excited. They could send children or elderly people flying, but not on purpose. Given enough exercise, they can be calm and affectionate pets and respond eagerly to commands once they know what to do.

ORIGINALLY BRED for pointing and retrieving on land and water.

Special characteristics
This dog is playful, energetic and good-tempered.

Exercise requirements
High. Full of energy, which needs to be channelled.

Attitude to

OWNERS responsive, affectionate
CHILDREN good-natured. May be too boisterous for very young children
OTHER PETS care with small animals
STRANGERS friendly
UNFAMILIAR DOGS friendly

Perfect owner
Energetic families who are active and busy, who want a dog to play with, run with, walk and train.

Potential problems
If not given sufficient exercise this dog may be boisterous and may run away.

Italian Spinone

faithful • responsive • patient • affectionate • easy-going • biddable

SIZE **60–70 cm (23–27½ in)** • WEIGHT **29–39 kg (64–86 lb)** • COAT **Tough, thick, slightly wiry** • COLOUR **White, white with orange markings, solid white peppered orange, white with brown markings, white speckled with brown (brown roan), with or without large brown markings** • LIFESPAN **12–14 years**

The Spinone is a popular dog with families because of its easy-going, good nature. Exuberantly playful during the excitement of a walk, they are calm and gentle at home.

ORIGINALLY BRED for retrieval of game and tracking.

Special characteristics
The Spinone is calm and playful, with a 'soft' mouth and is interested in scents.

Exercise requirements
High–Medium. Energetic outside, but content to rest at home.

Attitude to
OWNERS **biddable, enjoys close bond**
CHILDREN **patient, good-natured**
OTHER PETS **good**
STRANGERS **friendly, can be cautious**
UNFAMILIAR DOGS **friendly**

Perfect owner
Families who enjoy long walks, likes to play games with their dog and want a close companion.

Potential problems
This breed may suffer from separation problems.

⚠ Regular face-washing is essential to keep this dog's beard and whiskers sweet-smelling.

Gundogs

Kooikerhondje

sensitive • good-natured • alert

SIZE 35–40 cm (14–16 in) • WEIGHT 9–11 kg (20–24 lb) • COAT Medium long, slightly waved or straight • COLOUR Clear orange-red coloured patches on white • LIFESPAN 12–13 years

Gundogs

These attractive dogs are both energetic and busy. Cautious with strangers, these loyal dogs like to build strong bonds with their owners. They are sensitive and industrious and like to have something to do to keep them occupied.

ORIGINALLY BRED as a decoy to lure ducks and for flushing and retrieval.

Special characteristics
The Kooikerhondje has a lively, active mind that needs stimulation.

Exercise requirements
High. Energetic, enjoys being busy.

Attitude to
OWNERS friendly, loyal
CHILDREN good-natured if brought up with them
OTHER PETS good
STRANGERS cautious but friendly
UNFAMILIAR DOGS cautious but friendly

Perfect owner
Active, gentle family or owner who is happy to play with their dog and wants a close companion.

⚠ This dog's feathers will bring in mud and dirt from outside.

Large Munsterlander

alert • energetic • keen worker • biddable • loyal • affectionate • trustworthy

SIZE **58–65 cm (23–25½ in)** • WEIGHT **25–29 kg (55–65 lb)** • COAT Hair long and dense, but not curly or coarse. Well feathered on front and hind legs and on tail • COLOUR Head solid black. Body white or blue roan with black patches, flecked, ticked, or combination of these • LIFESPAN 12–13 years

Loyalty to their owners comes high on the Munsterlander's list of priorities, with exercise a close second. These strong-willed dogs are full of energy and will play games all day if they can. The Small Munsterlander is a different breed that looks similar, but is smaller, and the coat is liver instead of black.

ORIGINALLY BRED as a colour variation of the German Wirehaired Pointer for tracking, pointing and retrieving on land and in water.

Special characteristics
This dog is energetic and playful, and interested in scents.

Exercise requirements
High. Needs exercise both inside and outside the house.

Attitude to
OWNERS biddable, loyal
CHILDREN usually tolerant, may be too boisterous for young children
OTHER PETS good
STRANGERS usually good if well socialized
UNFAMILIAR DOGS usually friendly

Perfect owner
Experienced, active owner who can set clear guidelines for behaviour and provide plenty of activity, play and training.

Potential problems
Some lines can be strong-willed and prone to status-related aggression with gentle owners, and unless well socialized may see strangers as a threat.

Gundogs

⚠ This dog's feathers will bring in mud and dirt from outside.

Gundogs

Spanish Water Dog

faithful • obedient • brave • good-tempered • watchful

SIZE **40–50 cm (15½–19½ in)** • WEIGHT **14–22 kg (30–48 lb)** • COAT Curled woolly texture, forming cords when long. Needs to be clipped • COLOUR Solid black, brown or white of various shades; black and white or brown and white (particolour) but never tricoloured • LIFESPAN 10–14 years

With its distinctive curly coat, this dog is loyal and likes to bond closely to its owners. It is a natural guard and is aloof or territorial with strangers. A hard-working, willing dog, it needs plenty of activity to be happy.

ORIGINALLY BRED to work with fishermen and for herding and retrieving.

Special characteristics
Responsive to commands, the Spanish Water Dog is playful and energetic, and likes to swim.

Exercise requirements
High. Needs plenty of exercise.

Attitude to
OWNERS loyal and close bonding
CHILDREN can be intolerant
OTHER PETS may be problematic with small pets
STRANGERS natural guard, territorial
UNFAMILIAR DOGS usually good

Perfect owner
Experienced owner who wants an unusual breed and who can cope with the high energy level and the need to provide daily interest through play, socializing, training and activity.

Potential problems
If not properly socialized, may display territorial aggression to strangers.

Weimaraner

friendly • exuberant • protective • obedient • active • alert

SIZE **56–69 cm (22–27 in)** • WEIGHT **32–39 kg (70½–86 lb)** • COAT Short, smooth and sleek. (There is also a long-haired variety.) • COLOUR Preferably silver-grey, shades of mouse or roe-grey permissible. Whole coat gives an appearance of metallic sheen • LIFESPAN **13 years**

Weimaraners are exuberant and energetic. They thrive on action and enjoy curling up with their family after a long day's activity. Their good nature makes them excellent family dogs, but their enthusiasm can make them clumsy enough to knock over or squash things more delicate than themselves.

ORIGINALLY BRED to track large game, then to hunt, point and retrieve.

Special characteristics
Active, exuberant and playful, the Weimeraner develops close bonds with its owner. It can be stubborn.

Exercise requirements
Very high. Needs plenty of exercise, particularly when young.

Attitude to
OWNERS attentive, tactile
CHILDREN good, may be too boisterous for small children
OTHER PETS good, but may chase or squash
STRANGERS good if well socialized, can be territorial
UNFAMILIAR DOGS friendly if well socialized

Perfect owner
Energetic strong-willed owner who enjoys playing, training and being very active.

Potential problems
Lack of exercise can result in boisterousness, running away or destructiveness. May be aggressive to other dogs unless properly socialized.

⚠ The Weimaraner's sleek coat is thin and they can suffer from the cold if left outside.

Wirehaired Pointing Griffon

friendly • dependable • sensitive • energetic

SIZE 56–61 cm (22–24 in) • WEIGHT 23–27 kg (50–60 lb) • COAT Thick, medium length, wiry • COLOUR Steel grey with brown markings • LIFESPAN 12–15 years

Gundogs

Energetic Wirehaired Pointing Griffons are sensitive and hardworking. Responsive and close bonding, they enjoy gentle, active families, and have enough energy to play all day and be ready for action again the next morning.

ORIGINALLY BRED for hunting and retrieving on land and water.

Attitude to

OWNERS affectionate, responsive
CHILDREN good
OTHER PETS good, may chase
STRANGERS friendly
UNFAMILIAR DOGS friendly

Perfect owner
Active families who enjoy energetic walks, playing and training and who want a close bond with their dog.

Potential problems
Some submissive urination in females, especially if they are handled harshly.

Special characteristics
This breed is playful and exuberant, and enjoys scenting and flushing out wildlife.

Exercise requirements
High. Needs plenty of opportunities to run.

⚠ This dog's facial hair needs frequent washing to keep it clean.

Pointer

gentle • obedient • sensitive • alert • kind

SIZE 61–69 cm (24–27 in) • WEIGHT 20–30 kg (44–66 lb) • COAT Fine, short, hard • COLOUR Lemon and white, orange and white, liver and white, and black and white • LIFESPAN 12–14 years

Long-legged and agile, the energetic Pointer needs plenty of exercise to stay calm at home where it will be affectionate and good-natured with its family. These dogs possess a great sense of smell and enjoy long, active, nose-to-the-ground walks.

ORIGINALLY BRED to flush and point to game.

Special characteristics
Playful and active, the Pointer is particularly interested in scents.

Exercise requirements
High. Needs regular, long walks.

Attitude to
OWNERS affectionate, biddable
CHILDREN tolerant, gentle, but may be too boisterous for very young children
OTHER PETS good
STRANGERS friendly
UNFAMILIAR DOGS friendly

Perfect owner
Kind, playful, sociable families who enjoy an active life with plenty of long, energetic walks and who can provide games and activities to keep this breed occupied.

Gundogs

German Shorthaired Pointer

gentle • affectionate • even-tempered • alert • biddable • loyal

SIZE **53–64 cm (21–25 in)** • WEIGHT **27–32 kg (60–70 lb)** • COAT Short, flat and slightly coarse to touch • COLOUR Solid liver, liver and white spotted, liver and white spotted and ticked, liver and white ticked, solid black, or black and white • LIFESPAN 14–16 years

Gundogs

Enthusiastic German Shorthaired Pointers are full of life and vigour. Tolerant, responsive and easy-going by nature, they make excellent family pets providing they have an outlet for their abundant energy.

ORIGINALLY BRED for flushing and pointing at game.

Special characteristics
Obedient and playful, this dog is very interested in scents.

Exercise requirements
High. Needs energetic walks.

Attitude to
OWNERS affectionate, biddable
CHILDREN good, may be too boisterous for young children
OTHER PETS good, may chase
STRANGERS friendly
UNFAMILIAR DOGS friendly

Perfect owner
Active, sociable, affectionate families who enjoy energetic walks and games with their dog.

Potential problems
Needs plenty of exercise or may become boisterous or destructive, or run away.

German Wirehaired Pointer

gentle • affectionate • even-tempered • alert • biddable • loyal

SIZE **56–67 cm (22–26½ in)** • WEIGHT **20.5–34 kg (45–75 lb)** • COAT **Outer coat thick and harsh with a dense undercoat** • COLOUR **Liver and white, solid liver, black and white** • LIFESPAN **10–12 years**

A little more strong-willed than the shorthaired version, the Wirehaired Pointer is energetic, affectionate and good-natured. These dogs have energy in abundance and they need homes where long walks and action are part of the package.

ORIGINALLY BRED for flushing and pointing at game.

Special characteristics
Obedient and playful, the Wirehaired Pointer is interested in scents.

Exercise requirements
High. Needs long walks to burn off abundant energy.

Attitude to
OWNERS affectionate, biddable
CHILDREN good, may be too boisterous for young children
OTHER PETS good, may chase
STRANGERS friendly
UNFAMILIAR DOGS friendly

Perfect owner
Active, sociable, affectionate families who enjoy energetic walks and games with their dog.

Potential problems
Needs plenty of exercise or may become boisterous or destructive, or run away.

Gundogs

Chesapeake Bay Retriever

independent • affectionate • courageous • strong-willed • alert • responsive

SIZE 53–66 cm (21–26 in) • WEIGHT 32–36 kg (70–80 lb) • COAT Coat thick and reasonably short with harsh oily outer coat • COLOUR Dead grass (straw to bracken), sedge (red gold), or any shade of brown • LIFESPAN 12–13 years

Chesapeakes will defend you with their lives, but need careful, experienced handling to ensure humans stay in control. These strong, active dogs have a coat that protects them from cold water so swimming is just one of the energetic activities they enjoy.

ORIGINALLY BRED in the USA for retrieving waterfowl.

Special characteristics
Playful and active, this retriever particularly enjoys swimming.

Exercise requirements
High. Full of energy that needs to be channelled.

Attitude to
OWNERS loyal, affectionate
CHILDREN good-natured if raised with them, can be intolerant
OTHER PETS good
STRANGERS usually good if well socialized, can be territorial
UNFAMILIAR DOGS usually good, can be territorial

Perfect owner
Strong-willed, experienced, active owner who enjoys long energetic walks, playing retrieve games and plenty of training.

Potential problems
May display status-related aggression towards gentle owners. May be aggressive to strangers if not properly socialized.

Gundogs

Curly Coated Retriever

bold • friendly • self-confident • independent • aloof • enthusiastic • curious

SIZE **64–69 cm (25–27 in)** • WEIGHT **32–36 kg (70–80 lb)** • COAT **Body coat a thick mass of small tight, crisp curls lying close to skin, short coat on face. Coat sheds** • COLOUR **Black or liver** • LIFESPAN **12–13 years**

Independent, but affectionate and playful, these retrievers are loyal to their families, but are not quite so keen on strangers. Their distinctive curly coats protect them from cold and rain so they will be always ready for long active walks whatever the weather.

ORIGINALLY BRED for retrieving waterfowl.

Attitude to
OWNERS **affectionate, tactile**
CHILDREN **good, may be too boisterous for young children**
OTHER PETS **good**
STRANGERS **reserved**
UNFAMILIAR DOGS **good**

Perfect owner
Active, confident owner who wants to play games and enjoy long energetic walks.

Potential problems
If not properly socialized, may be aggressive to strangers.

Special characteristics
This retriever is playful and active, and loves to swim.

Exercise requirements
High. Very active and needs regular, long walks.

Gundogs

Flat Coated Retriever

happy • kind • optimistic • friendly • active

SIZE **56–61 cm (22–24 in)** • WEIGHT **25–36 kg (55–80 lb)** • COAT **Dense, fine, flat. Legs and tail well feathered** • COLOUR **Black or liver only** • LIFESPAN **11–13 years**

Gundogs

Flat Coated Retrievers are affectionate, lively and playful. Sociable, friendly and interested in everything, and responsive to requests, they make ideal family pets for active owners.

ORIGINALLY BRED for retrieving game on land and in water.

Special characteristics
Active and playful, the Flat Coated Retriever loves to swim.

Exercise requirements
High. Full of energy outside, calmer in the house.

Attitude to
OWNERS **affectionate, biddable**
CHILDREN **good**
OTHER PETS **good**
STRANGERS **friendly**
UNFAMILIAR DOGS **friendly**

Perfect owner
Active, affectionate, sociable families who enjoy energetic walks, and playing games with their dog.

✓ Recommended for energetic, first-time owners, but it is important to find a dog from a healthy line.

⚠ These retrievers will bring in mud and dirt from outside on the feathers.

Golden Retriever

biddable • relaxed • kind • friendly • confident • responsive • sensible

SIZE **51–61 cm (20–24 in)** • WEIGHT **27–36 kg (60–80 lb)** • COAT **Flat or wavy with good feathering**
• COLOUR **Any shade of gold or cream** • LIFESPAN **12–13 years**

A popular family dog for good reason, Golden Retrievers are good-natured, playful and kind. These dogs are people enthusiasts and are just as happy greeting people at the door with a shoe in their mouths as they are retrieving game in the fields.

ORIGINALLY BRED for retrieving game on land and in water.

Special characteristics
The Golden Retriever is active and playful, and likes to swim.

Exercise requirements
High. Enjoys long walks and lots of games.

Attitude to
OWNERS affectionate, biddable
CHILDREN patient
OTHER PETS good
STRANGERS friendly
UNFAMILIAR DOGS friendly

Perfect owner
Active, affectionate, sociable families who enjoy energetic walks and playing with their dog.

Potential problems
Some lines may display aggressive possession-guarding.

⚠ This dog will bring in mud and dirt from outside on its feathers.

Gundogs

Gundogs

Labradors

The friendly, good-natured Labrador is well known and well loved everywhere. Whether trained to provide assistance to disabled people or giving love and affection in a family home, this versatile dog is a playful, happy enthusiast.

Yellow/Black/Chocolate

kind • responsive • keen • biddable • enthusiastic • affable

SIZE **55–57 cm (21½–22½ in)** • WEIGHT **25–34 kg (55–75 lb)** • COAT **Short, dense, without wave or feathering** • COLOUR **Yellow, black or chocolate** • LIFESPAN **12–13 years**

ORIGINALLY BRED to help fisherman bring in their nets, later for flushing and retrieving game.

Special characteristics
Active and playful, the Labrador loves to swim.

Exercise requirements
Very high. Needs regular long walks and play sessions.

Attitude to
OWNERS **affectionate, biddable**
CHILDREN **patient**
OTHER PETS **good**
STRANGERS **friendly**
UNFAMILIAR DOGS **friendly**

Perfect owner
Active, affectionate, sociable, exuberant families who can provide enough energetic walks, plenty of play and active training routines.

Potential problems
Often destructive chewers during adolescence. Lack of exercise may lead to boisterousness, running away and destructive behaviour.

✔ Recommended for energetic, first-time owners. Its good nature makes the Labrador an ideal family pet.

Yellow and Black Labradors

Yellow Labradors (opposite) tend to have a slightly softer temperament than the Blacks (right) and are more likely to be easy going. Both can be bred for working or show purposes, and it may be best to choose one from a show line rather than from working stock unless you are prepared for lots of exercise.

Chocolate Labradors

Chocolate Labradors tend to be more tolerant to pain and, consequently, often injure themselves more readily. They can be more exhuberant and enthusiastic, and are prone to running headlong into their owners, strangers or other dogs. This can cause problems with some people and other dogs who are unlikely to tolerate such impudence from others.

Nova Scotia Duck-tolling Retriever

kind • confident • responsive • sensitive • easy to train • playful • active

SIZE 45–51 cm (18–20 in) • WEIGHT 17–23 kg (37–51 lb) • COAT Straight, double coat of medium/long length • COLOUR All shades of red or orange with lighter featherings and underside of tail • LIFESPAN 12–13 years

Gundogs

Nova Scotia Duck-tolling Retrievers were bred to lure ducks towards the hunts by leaping and playing by the water's edge, and then to retrieve them once shot. Energetic and playful, they need plenty of activity to keep them well exercised.

ORIGINALLY BRED to act as a decoy and to retrieve waterfowl.

Attitude to
OWNERS affectionate, biddable
CHILDREN good
OTHER PETS good, may chase
STRANGERS reserved
UNFAMILIAR DOGS friendly

Perfect owner
Active, affectionate families who enjoy energetic walks and can spend a great deal of time training and playing with this active breed.

Special characteristics
This retriever has an active, playful and curious nature.

Exercise requirements
Very high. Enjoys plenty of exercise and play sessions.

⚠️ This dog will bring in mud and dirt from outside on its feathers.

English Setter

graceful • able • outgoing • kind • very active • friendly • good-natured

SIZE 61–69 cm (24–27 in) • WEIGHT 25–30 kg (55–66 lb) • COAT Slightly wavy, not curly, long and silky • COLOUR Black and white (blue belton), orange and white (orange belton), lemon and white (lemon belton), liver and white (liver belton) or tricolour • LIFESPAN 12–13 years

English Setters are graceful and elegant in motion and like to run free to use up excess energy. Although affectionate and good-natured with their families, they are independent and are not always easy to train or responsive to requests.

ORIGINALLY BRED for flushing and retrieving birds.

Special characteristics
This setter is very active and exuberant.

Exercise requirements
High. Needs long walks on a regular basis.

⚠ This dog will bring in mud and dirt from outside on its feathers.

Attitude to
OWNERS affectionate, easy-going
CHILDREN good, may knock over young children
OTHER PETS good
STRANGERS friendly
UNFAMILIAR DOGS friendly

Perfect owner
Patient, affectionate, easy-going families with access to places where this dog can have plenty of freedom to run.

Gundogs

Gordon Setter

relaxed • friendly • devoted • loyal • stubborn

SIZE 62–66 cm (24½–26 in) • WEIGHT 25.5–29.5 kg (56–65 lb) • COAT Medium length; flat, with heavy feathering on legs and underside of body • COLOUR Black, with markings of chestnut red • LIFESPAN 12–14 years

Gundogs

Exuberant and lively, the Gordon Setter is affectionate and easy-going. These dogs love to run and need plenty of long, active walks. Their affectionate and devoted good nature makes up for their lack of responsiveness to requests.

ORIGINALLY BRED for flushing birds.

Special characteristics
The exuberant Gordon Setter enjoys being very active.

Exercise requirements
Very high. Needs to be taken for long runs.

Attitude to
OWNERS affectionate, easy-going
CHILDREN good, may knock over young children
OTHER PETS good, may chase
STRANGERS friendly
UNFAMILIAR DOGS friendly

Perfect owner
Patient, affectionate, easy-going, strong-willed families with access to places where this dog can have plenty of freedom to run.

Potential problems
May display some status-related aggression with gentle owners. Lack of exercise may lead to escapes and running away.

⚠ This dog will bring in mud and dirt from outside on its feathers.

Irish Setter

exuberant • tremendously active • affectionate • excitable

SIZE 64–69 cm (25–27 in) • WEIGHT 27–32 kg (60–70 lb) • COAT Fine, flat and of medium length. Feathers on legs, feet, belly and tail • COLOUR Rich chestnut • LIFESPAN 12–13 years

Irish Setters were born to run. They have a natural exuberance and energy as well as an easy-going, good nature that fits in well with active families. Independent but affectionate, this dog is not given to responding readily to requests.

ORIGINALLY BRED for flushing and retrieving game.

Attitude to

OWNERS affectionate, easy-going
CHILDREN good, may knock over young children
OTHER PETS good, may chase
STRANGERS friendly
UNFAMILIAR DOGS friendly

Perfect owner
Patient, affectionate, easy-going families with access to places where this dog can have plenty of freedom to run.

Potential problems
Lack of exercise may lead to escapes, running away and hyperactivity.

Special characteristics
The Irish Setter is a very active, energetic and exuberant dog.

Exercise requirements
High. Needs long runs to burn off abundant energy.

⚠️ This dog will bring in mud and dirt from outside on its feathers.

Gundogs

Irish Red and White Setter

biddable • sensitive • good-natured • affectionate

SIZE **58–69 cm (23–27 in)** • WEIGHT **27–32 kg (60–70 lb)** • COAT **Fine, medium length with good feathering** • COLOUR **Clearly particoloured, base colour pearl white, solid red patches** • LIFESPAN **12–13 years**

Gundogs

The sensitive Irish Red and White Setter is reserved with strangers, but easy-going and affectionate to its family. Not known for being responsive to owners' requests, these dogs have a natural exuberance and energy that requires an outlet in the form of long walks and free running.

ORIGINALLY BRED for flushing and retrieving game.

Special characteristics
This setter is a very active and exuberant dog.

Exercise requirements
High. Full of energy and needs long runs.

Attitude to
OWNERS affectionate, easy-going
CHILDREN good, may knock over young children
OTHER PETS good, may chase
STRANGERS friendly or reserved
UNFAMILIAR DOGS friendly

Perfect owner
Patient, gentle, affectionate, easy-going families with access to places where this dog can have plenty of freedom to run.

Potential problems
Lack of exercise may lead to escapes, running away and hyperactivity. Can be shy with strangers unless well socialized.

⚠ This dog will bring in mud and dirt from outside on its feathers.

American Cocker Spaniel

happy • keen • affable • gentle • sometimes stubborn

SIZE 34–39 cm (13½–15½ in) • WEIGHT 11–13 kg (24–28 lb) • COAT Silky, medium length. Ears, chest, abdomen and legs well feathered • COLOUR Black, buff, red, chocolate; black, red or chocolate with white • LIFESPAN 12–14 years • ALSO KNOWN AS Cocker Spaniel

American Cocker Spaniels are dogs for owners who like to groom, walk and play. They are happy little characters that can be unresponsive to requests at times, but they have a joyful, playful nature that easily wins people over.

ORIGINALLY BRED for retrieving small game.

Special characteristics
This active and playful spaniel is always busy.

Exercise requirements
High. Enjoys walks and plenty of play sessions.

Attitude to
OWNERS affectionate, loyal
CHILDREN good if well socialized
OTHER PETS good
STRANGERS friendly
UNFAMILIAR DOGS friendly

Perfect owner
Active, affectionate families who enjoy energetic walks, playing and training and who have plenty of time and energy for coat care.

Potential problems
May display some status-related aggression problems with gentle owners, and food and possession-guarding. Dogs from some lines can be shy.

These dogs have been bred to have a head that is higher and more domed than the English Cocker Spaniel.

Gundogs

⚠ This spaniel's coat will bring in mud and dirt from outside. Daily brushing and coat care are needed to keep it in good condition.

American Water Spaniel

active • alert • responsive • outgoing • enthusiastic • sensitive

SIZE **36–46 cm (15–18 in)** • WEIGHT **11–20 kg (25–45 lb)** • COAT **Dense, curled** • COLOUR **Liver, brown, dark chocolate** • LIFESPAN **12–14 years**

Gundogs

American Water Spaniels are not very common, but they make enthusiastic, active pets. Finding an outlet for their energy is essential, as is socializing them with other dogs and children.

ORIGINALLY BRED for flushing and retrieving waterfowl.

Special characteristics
This active and playful spaniel loves to swim.

Exercise requirements
High. Needs plenty of exercise to burn off abundant energy.

Attitude to
OWNERS affectionate, loyal
CHILDREN good when socialized
with them
OTHER PETS good
STRANGERS friendly if well socialized
UNFAMILIAR DOGS can be problematic

Perfect owner
Active, experienced families who enjoy energetic walks, playing and training, and who can provide plenty of early socialization with other dogs.

Potential problems
Lack of exercise may lead to boisterousness, destructiveness and other behaviour problems. Has a tendency to jump up, and is occasionally possessive over food and toys.

Cocker Spaniel (English)

happy • affectionate • busy • exuberant • wilful

SIZE 38–41 cm (15–16 in) • WEIGHT 13–14.5 kg (28–32 lb) • COAT Flat, silky, medium length, well-feathered forelegs, body and hind legs • COLOUR Black, liver or red; white with black, blue, liver or red markings, roaning or ticking • LIFESPAN 12–14 years • ALSO KNOWN AS English Cocker Spaniel

As a puppy, the Cocker Spaniel is a cute bundle of fluff and many owners do not expect the wilful nature that appears later. Happy, exuberant and full of energy, they need plenty of exercise, together with strong-willed, active owners.

ORIGINALLY BRED for flushing and retrieving small game.

Special characteristics
Energetic and playful, the Cocker Spaniel is interested in scents and independent when outside.

Exercise requirements
High. Needs energetic walks as well as play sessions.

Attitude to
OWNERS affectionate, loyal
CHILDREN tolerant if well socialized
OTHER PETS good if raised with them
STRANGERS friendly but reserved
UNFAMILIAR DOGS friendly

Perfect owner
Active, strong-willed, sociable owner who enjoys energetic walks, playing and training.

Potential problems
May display status-related aggression, particularly prevalent in dogs of solid colours. Possessive aggression is also common.

⚠ The feathery coat will carry in mud and dirt from outside. The coat and long hairy ears require daily care to keep them in good healthy condition.

Gundogs

Clumber Spaniel

stoical • responsive • determined • reliable • kind • aloof • gentle • stubborn

SIZE **48–51 cm (19–20 in)** • WEIGHT **29–36 kg (65–80 lb)** • COAT **Abundant, silky and straight. Legs and chest well feathered** • COLOUR **Plain white body with lemon or orange markings** • LIFESPAN **12–13 years**

Gundogs

Clumber Spaniels are calm and steady with enough stamina to keep going all day, every day. They are silent workers who are loving and affectionate to owners and friendly with visitors.

ORIGINALLY BRED **for tracking and retrieving game.**

Special characteristics
This active spaniel is interested in scents.

Exercise requirements
Medium. Plenty of stamina for long walks.

Attitude to
OWNERS **affectionate, loyal**
CHILDREN **good**
OTHER PETS **good**
STRANGERS **friendly**
UNFAMILIAR DOGS **friendly**

Perfect owner
Steady, tolerant, social owner who enjoys long, quiet walks.

Potential problems
Under-exercised Clumbers may be destructive.

Dropping lower eyelids are common in this breed and care is needed to prevent injury or infection.

Field Spaniel

docile • affectionate • enthusiastic • active • sensitive • even-tempered

SIZE 43–46 cm (17–18 in) • WEIGHT 18–25 kg (40–55 lb) • COAT Long, flat, glossy and silky in texture. Abundant feathering on chest, under body and behind legs • COLOUR Black, liver or roan. Any one of these with tan markings • LIFESPAN 12–13 years

✔ Recommended for energetic, first-time owners. It is important to find a healthy dog.

⚠ The silky coat requires daily grooming to keep it in good condition, and the long hairy ears need special attention.

Affectionate, happy and eager to please, Field Spaniels make entertaining, enthusiastic companions. They are easily trained and friendly and make ideal pets for active, playful families.

ORIGINALLY BRED for retrieving game.

Special characteristics
The Field Spaniel is active, playful and enthusiastic.

Exercise requirements
High. Enjoys walks and games.

Attitude to
OWNERS affectionate, biddable
CHILDREN good
OTHER PETS good
STRANGERS friendly
UNFAMILIAR DOGS friendly

Perfect owner
Active, affectionate, sociable families who enjoy energetic walks and playing games with their dog.

Irish Water Spaniel

affectionate • gentle • aloof • staunch • responsive • playful

SIZE 51–58 cm (20–23 in) • WEIGHT 20–30 kg (45–65 lb) • COAT Dense, tight, crisp ringlets • COLOUR Rich, dark liver with purplish tint or bloom peculiar to the breed • LIFESPAN 13 years

Gundogs

Playful and friendly, the Irish Water Spaniel makes a good pet for energetic families. Finding an outlet for their exuberant energy is important and swimming is high on their list of things they love to do.

ORIGINALLY BRED for retrieving waterfowl.

Special characteristics

This spaniel is active, interested in scents and loves to swim when given the opportunity.

Exercise requirements

High. Needs energetic walks and enjoys swimming.

Attitude to

OWNERS affectionate, responsive
CHILDREN good
OTHER PETS good
STRANGERS friendly
UNFAMILIAR DOGS friendly

Perfect owner

Active, affectionate, sociable families who enjoy energetic walks and playing games with their dog.

Sussex Spaniel

kind • methodical • steady • determined

SIZE **38–41 cm (15–16 in)** • WEIGHT **18–23 kg (40–50 lb)** • COAT **Abundant and flat. Ears covered with soft, wavy hair. Forequarters and hindquarters moderately well feathered** • COLOUR **Rich golden liver and hair shading to golden at tip** • LIFESPAN **11–12 years**

Sussex Spaniels are calm and steady workers with plenty of stamina to keep going all day. At home they are affectionate and friendly and are less exuberant and boisterous than many other gundogs.

ORIGINALLY BRED for tracking and flushing game.

Special characteristics
Steady and active, this spaniel is interested in scents.

Exercise requirements
Medium. Enjoys long walks as has plenty of stamina.

Attitude to
OWNERS **affectionate, gentle**
CHILDREN **good**
OTHER PETS **good**
STRANGERS **friendly if well socialized**
UNFAMILIAR DOGS **friendly if well socialized**

Perfect owner
Steady, patient owner who enjoys long, quiet walks.

Gundogs

⚠ This dog's coat will bring in some mud and dirt from outside. Its long hairy ears need care. It has drooping lower eyelids that can result in eye infections.

English Springer Spaniel

active • enthusiastic • intense • friendly • happy • biddable

SIZE **46–48 cm (18–19 in)** • WEIGHT **16–20 kg (35–45 lb)** • COAT Close, straight, medium length. Moderate feathering on ears, forelegs, body and hindquarters • COLOUR Liver and white, black and white, or either of these colours with tan markings • LIFESPAN **12–14 years**

Gundogs

Vigorous, happy and enthusiastic, the English Springer Spaniel is renowned for its energetic, friendly approach to life. They like to be busy all day, and make good pets for active, lively families.

ORIGINALLY BRED for flushing (springing) and retrieving game.

Special characteristics
The English Springer Spaniel is energetic, playful and affectionate.

Exercise requirements
Very high. Has plenty of stamina for long walks.

Attitude to
OWNERS **affectionate, active**
CHILDREN **good**
OTHER PETS **good**
STRANGERS **friendly**
UNFAMILIAR DOGS **friendly**

Perfect owner
Active, affectionate, sociable families who enjoy energetic walks and like to play and train every day.

⚠ This dog's coat will bring in mud and dirt from outside, and needs daily attention. Its long hairy ears also need care to keep them in good condition.

Welsh Springer Spaniel

strong • athletic • happy • very active • kind • responsive • determined

SIZE **46–48 cm (18–19 in)** • WEIGHT **16–20 kg (35–45 lb)** • COAT **Straight or flat, silky texture, medium length. Forelegs and hind legs above hocks moderately feathered, ears and tail lightly feathered** • COLOUR **Rich red and white only** • LIFESPAN **12–14 years**

A little more wilful than the English, the Welsh Springer Spaniel has just as much energy and enthusiasm for life. Happy and active, they need plenty of play and long walks to prevent them being boisterous in the house.

ORIGINALLY BRED for flushing (springing) and retrieving game

Special characteristics
This spaniel has an active, playful and curious nature.

Exercise requirements
Very high. Enjoys long walks and plenty of play.

Attitude to
OWNERS **affectionate**
CHILDREN **friendly**
OTHER PETS **good**
STRANGERS **friendly**
UNFAMILIAR DOGS **friendly if well socialized**

Perfect owner
Active, experienced, strong-willed owner who enjoys long, energetic walks and who likes to play and train regularly.

Potential problems
May have status-related problems with gentle owners. Possessive aggression and aggression towards other dogs sometimes occur.

⚠ This dog will bring in mud and dirt from outside on the feathers.

Gundogs

Afghan Hound

dignified • aloof • keen • graceful • elegant • sensitive

SIZE **63–74 cm (25–29 in)** • WEIGHT **23–27 kg (50–60 lb)** • COAT **Very long and very fine** • COLOUR **All colours acceptable** • LIFESPAN **12–14 years**

Hounds

Afghans look lovely when fully groomed, but it can take a long time every day to look after their coats. These elegant, independent dogs need regular energetic runs in a safe area.

ORIGINALLY BRED for chasing large game such as deer and leopard by running ahead of hunters.

Special characteristics
This swift-moving dog has an independent character.

Exercise requirements
High. Needs energetic runs, although lazy at home.

Attitude to
OWNERS **affectionate, independent**
CHILDREN **tolerant, aloof**
OTHER PETS **may be problematic with small pets**
STRANGERS **indifferent, aloof**
UNFAMILIAR DOGS **playful**

Perfect owner
Patient owner who has time for the considerable coat maintenance, who wants a dog with an independent spirit and who can provide adequate space for several fast runs a day. For people who do not want a close bond with their dog.

Potential problems
Prone to running away to chase other animals when off lead.

⚠ Daily care of the coat is needed to keep it in good condition, and de-tangling takes time.

Basenji

quiet • independent • affectionate • aloof • alert • docile

SIZE 40–43 cm (16–17 in) • WEIGHT 9.5–11 kg (21–24 lb) • COAT Short, sleek, very fine. Easily cleaned • COLOUR Red and white, tan and white, black and white, brindle. White legs, blaze and white collar optional • LIFESPAN 12 years

Developed as a hunting dog in the Congo, Basenjis do not bark, but instead make a yodelling sound when excited. They are clean and neat, being almost cat-like with an independent, aloof nature.

ORIGINALLY BRED as a general-purpose hunting dog.

Special characteristics
This barkless breed is clean and curious.

Exercise requirements
Medium. Needs energetic walks.

Attitude to
OWNERS independent, spirited
CHILDREN good
OTHER PETS may be problematic with small pets
STRANGERS reserved then friendly
UNFAMILIAR DOGS playful

Perfect owner
Easy-going owner who requires an independent, sweet-natured, cat-like dog to take for energetic walks.

Potential problems
May be difficult to control on walks.

Hounds

Basset Fauve de Bretagne

courageous • hardy • lively • friendly • amiable • tenacious

SIZE **32–38 cm (12½–15 in)** • WEIGHT **16–18 kg (36–40 lb)** • COAT **Very harsh, dense and flat** • COLOUR **Fawn, gold-wheaten or red-wheaten** • LIFESPAN **12–14 years**

Hounds

Easy-going and cheerful, the Basset Fauve de Bretagne thrives on exercise and needs plenty of long, active walks. This dog is affectionate and friendly, but independent, with a mind and opinion of its own.

ORIGINALLY BRED for hunting rabbits and hares in a pack ahead of hunters on foot.

Special characteristics
An active, curious and very friendly hound.

Exercise requirements
Medium. Needs regular, long walks.

Attitude to
OWNERS affectionate, independent
children good
OTHER PETS generally good,
may chase
STRANGERS friendly
UNFAMILIAR DOGS playful

Perfect owner
Easy-going, active, affectionate owner who enjoys long, energetic walks with this cheerful, independent little dog.

Potential problems
May be difficult to control on walks.

Basset Hound

placid • affectionate • stubborn • gentle

SIZE **33–38 cm (13–15 in)** • WEIGHT **18–27 kg (40–60 lb)** • COAT **Smooth, short** • COLOUR **Generally black, white and tan (tricolour); lemon and white (bicolour)** • LIFESPAN **12 years**

Basset Hounds are placid and calm and friendly to all, but can be stubbornly independent when asked to do something. Affectionate and placid, they are very interested in scents when outside, which can make walks difficult.

ORIGINALLY BRED for hunting rabbits and hares.

Special characteristics

An independent character, the Bassett is particularly interested in scents.

Exercise requirements

Medium. Needs steady exercise.

Attitude to

OWNERS **affectionate, independent**
CHILDREN **good**
OTHER PETS **good**
STRANGERS **friendly**
UNFAMILIAR DOGS **friendly**

Perfect owner

Patient, easy-going owner who will enjoy the independent character of these friendly but solemn hounds.

Hounds

Breeders have exaggerated the ear length of this dog so special care is needed to ensure they are kept clean and free from damage.

⚠ This dog has drooping lower eyelids that can result in eye infections. Ears and low slung body will carry dirt into the house. Heavy jowls cause lack of saliva control.

Beagle

bold • friendly • very active • determined • alert • curious • amiable

SIZE **33–40 cm (13–16 in)** • WEIGHT **8–14 kg (18–30 lb)** • COAT **Short, dense** • COLOUR **Any recognized hound colour other than liver. Tip of tail white** • LIFESPAN **13 years**

Hounds

Happy and full of life, Beagles have a lovely, tolerant nature. They also have an independent spirit and their strong desire to follow a scent can make them resistant to their owner's calls on walks.

ORIGINALLY BRED for hunting hares and rabbits in packs, with hunters following on foot.

Special characteristics
Active and independent, the Beagle is very interested in scents.

Exercise requirements
High. Needs plenty of walks, but little exercise at home.

Attitude to
OWNERS **independent, affectionate**
CHILDREN **good**
OTHER PETS **good, but may chase**
STRANGERS **friendly**
UNFAMILIAR DOGS **friendly**

Perfect owner
Easy-going, affectionate owner who enjoys energetic walks.

Potential problems
May be difficult to control on walks. Can be vocal if bored.

Bloodhound

affectionate • friendly • reserved • sensitive • affable • stubborn

SIZE 58–69 cm (23–27 in) • WEIGHT 36–50 kg (100–110 lb) • COAT Smooth, short • COLOUR Black and tan, liver and tan (red and tan), and red • LIFESPAN 10 years

Bloodhounds are gentle giants. Their ability to follow a scent is legendary and they need very long walks on a lead or in a safe area. Affectionate and good-natured, they can be stubborn and independent when it suits them.

ORIGINALLY BRED to track scent trails.

Special characteristics
The Bloodhound has been bred to be very interested in scents.

Exercise requirements
Low. Will, however, need long walks.

Attitude to
OWNERS independent, affectionate
CHILDREN good, may knock over young children
OTHER PETS good
STRANGERS friendly
UNFAMILIAR DOGS friendly

Perfect owner
Easy-going owner who has enough space for a large dog with a sweeping tail and who enjoys long walks at the end of a lead attached to a giant sniffing machine.

Potential problems
May be difficult to control on walks.

⚠ This dog's large loose jowls can lead to problems with saliva control.

Hounds

Black and Tan Coonhound

very active • alert • mellow • gentle • watchful • curious • affectionate

SIZE **58–69 cm (23–27 in)** • WEIGHT **23–34 kg (50–75 lb)** • COAT **Smooth, short, glossy**
• COLOUR **Black and tan** • LIFESPAN **11–12 years**

Hounds

Gentle, good-natured, affectionate Black and Tan Coonhounds are easy-going in the house. Outside they are independent, scent-orientated hunters and need long lead walks or a safe area where they can run free.

ORIGINALLY BRED to 'tree' raccoons or opossum until the hunter could catch up on foot.

Special characteristics
This hound is very interested in scents and hunting.

Extra long ears frame this dog's face and need special care.

Exercise requirements
High. Needs plenty of long walks, but little exercise at home.

Attitude to
OWNERS **independent, affectionate**
CHILDREN **good**
OTHER PETS **may be problematic with small pets**
STRANGERS **accepting**
UNFAMILIAR DOGS **friendly**

Perfect owner
Easy-going owner who wants a large, independent dog to take for long walks.

Potential problems
May be difficult to control on walks.

Borzoi

sensitive • alert • aloof • gentle • amenable

SIZE **68–74 cm (27–29 in)** • WEIGHT **35–48 kg (75–105 lb)** • COAT **Silky, flat, wavy or rather curly, long on body** • COLOUR **Any** • LIFESPAN **11–13 years**

Aloof, sensitive and elegant, the Borzoi is a gentle aristocrat. Independent and not very responsive to owners' wishes, outside they can transform into graceful running machines when allowed off-lead in safe areas, and enjoy chasing things they shouldn't.

ORIGINALLY BRED by the Russian aristocracy to course wolves in pairs.

Special characteristics
This elegant hound likes to chase.

Exercise requirements
Low. Needs brisk walks.

Attitude to
OWNERS **affectionate, independent**
CHILDREN **will tolerate**
OTHER PETS **good, may chase**
STRANGERS **indifferent**
UNFAMILIAR DOGS **friendly**

Perfect owner
Gentle, easy-going owner who will enjoy taking this elegant, independent dog for brisk walks.

Potential problems
May decide to chase instead of responding to owner's call.

Hounds

Borzois have a long distinctive Roman nose and narrow head.

Dachshunds

Dachshunds are gentle and sweet-natured. They like to be with people and their small size makes them easy to exercise. They can also be wilful and independent, preferring to do their own thing than comply with requests.

Long Haired

gentle • courageous • docile • outgoing • versatile • good-tempered

SIZE **20–25 cm (8–10 in)** • WEIGHT **6.5–11.5 kg (15–35 lb)** • COAT **Soft and straight long hair** • COLOUR **Any** • LIFESPAN **14–16 years**

ORIGINALLY BRED **to dig out badgers and foxes from their earths.**

Special characteristics
Independent and inquisitive, the dachshund likes to dig.

Exercise requirements
Low. Accepts exercise readily, but is not overdemanding.

Attitude to
OWNERS **independent, affectionate**
CHILDREN **good**
OTHER PETS **may be problematic with small pets**
STRANGERS **friendly**
UNFAMILIAR DOGS **friendly**

Perfect owner
Easy-going owner who will enjoy this independent, tough little dog and who is prepared to groom its long hair daily.

⚠ The dog's long hair will bring in mud and dirt from outside. Daily grooming is needed to keep it in good condition.

Smooth Haired

gentle • courageous • docile • outgoing • versatile • good-tempered

SIZE 20–25 cm (8–10 in) • WEIGHT 6.5–11.5 kg (15–35 lb) • COAT Dense, short, smooth • COLOUR Any
• LIFESPAN 14–16 years

ORIGINALLY BRED to dig out badgers and foxes from their earths.

Special characteristics
Independent and inquisitive, the dachshund likes to dig.

Exercise requirements
Low. Accepts exercise readily, but is not overdemanding.

Attitude to
OWNERS independent, affectionate
CHILDREN good
OTHER PETS may be problematic with small pets
STRANGERS friendly
UNFAMILIAR DOGS friendly

Perfect owner
Easy-going owner who will enjoy this independent, tough little dog.

Hounds

Wire Haired

gentle • courageous • docile • outgoing • versatile • good-tempered

SIZE **20–25 cm (8–10 in)** • WEIGHT **6.5–11.5 kg (15–35 lb)** • COAT **Short, straight, harsh coat with dense undercoat** • COLOUR **Any** • LIFESPAN **14–16 years**

Hounds

ORIGINALLY BRED to dig out badgers and foxes from their earths.

Special characteristics
Independent and inquisitive, the dachshund likes to dig.

Exercise requirements
Low. Accepts exercise readily, but is not overdemanding.

Attitude to
OWNERS **independent, affectionate**
CHILDREN **good**
OTHER PETS **may be problematic with small pets**
STRANGERS **friendly**
UNFAMILIAR DOGS **friendly**

Perfect owner
Easy-going owner who will enjoy this independent, tough little dog.

⚠ The dog's beard and whiskers will require frequent washing to keep them sweet-smelling.

Miniature Long Haired

gentle • courageous • docile • outgoing • versatile • good-tempered

SIZE 13–16 cm (5–6 in) • WEIGHT 4–5 kg (9–10 lb) • COAT Soft and straight long hair • COLOUR Any
• LIFESPAN 14–16 years

ORIGINALLY BRED to dig out rabbits from their earths.

Special characteristics
Independent and inquisitive, the dachshund likes to dig.

Exercise requirements
Low. Accepts exercise readily, but is not overdemanding.

Attitude to
OWNERS independent, affectionate
CHILDREN good, can be a risk with young children
OTHER PETS may be problematic with small pets
STRANGERS friendly
UNFAMILIAR DOGS friendly, can be a risk with large, boisterous dogs

Perfect owner
Easy-going owner who will enjoy this independent, tough little dog, and who is prepared for the daily grooming required.

Hounds

⚠ The dog's long hair will bring in mud and dirt from outside, so daily grooming is needed to keep it in good condition.

Miniature Smooth Haired

gentle • courageous • docile • outgoing • versatile • good-tempered

SIZE 13–16 cm (5–6 in) • WEIGHT 4–5 kg (9–10 lb) • COAT Dense, short, smooth • COLOUR Any
• LIFESPAN 14–16 years

Hounds

ORIGINALLY BRED to dig out rabbits from their earths.

Special characteristics
Independent and inquisitive, the dachshund likes to dig.

Exercise requirements
Low. Accepts exercise readily, but is not overdemanding.

Attitude to
OWNERS independent, affectionate
CHILDREN good, can be a risk with young children
OTHER PETS may be problematic with small pets
STRANGERS friendly
UNFAMILIAR DOGS friendly, can be a risk with large, boisterous dogs

Perfect owner
Easy-going owner who will enjoy this independent, tough little dog.

Miniature Wire Haired

gentle • courageous • docile • outgoing • versatile • good-tempered

SIZE **13–16 cm (5–6 in)** • WEIGHT **4–5 kg (9–10 lb)** • COAT **Short, straight, harsh coat with dense undercoat** • COLOUR **Any** • LIFESPAN **14–16 years**

ORIGINALLY BRED to dig out rabbits from their earths.

Special characteristics
Independent and inquisitive, the dachshund likes to dig.

Exercise requirements
Low. Accepts exercise readily, but is not overdemanding.

Attitude to
OWNERS independent, affectionate
CHILDREN good, can be a risk with young children
OTHER PETS may be problematic with small pets
STRANGERS friendly
UNFAMILIAR DOGS friendly, can be a risk with large, boisterous dogs

Perfect owner
Easy-going owner who will enjoy this independent, tough little dog.

⚠ The dog's beard and whiskers will require frequent washing to keep them sweet-smelling.

Hounds

Deerhound

gentle • calm • friendly • good-tempered • easy-going • independent

SIZE 71–76 cm (28–30 in) • WEIGHT 36.5–45.5 kg (80–100 lb) • COAT Shaggy, but not overcoated
• COLOUR Dark blue-grey, darker and lighter greys or brindles and yellows, sandy-red or red fawns with black points • LIFESPAN 10–11 years • ALSO KNOWN AS Scottish Deerhound

Hounds

Deerhounds enjoy long runs and are fast and elegant in motion. Independent and deaf to commands once on a chase, these sensitive, gentle dogs are calm and quiet in the house.

Attitude to
OWNERS independent, affectionate
CHILDREN good, will tolerate
OTHER PETS may be problematic with small pets
STRANGERS reserved but friendly
UNFAMILIAR DOGS friendly

Perfect owner
Gentle owner who will enjoy this independent, calm, graceful dog.

Potential problems
May be difficult to control on walks.

ORIGINALLY BRED for hunting deer in forests.

Special characteristics
The inquisitive Deerhound likes to run fast for short periods.

Exercise requirements
Low. Needs regular fast runs, but is quiet at home.

Elkhound

active • vocal • bold • independent • outgoing

SIZE 49–52 cm (19–21 in) • WEIGHT 20–23 kg (44–50 lb) • COAT Thick, short to medium length
• COLOUR Various shades of grey • LIFESPAN 12–13 years

Unlike many hounds, Elkhounds are vocal and strong-willed. They are independent, active hunters and own a coat that could protect them from the worst of weathers, but which can be problematic in a warm house and requires daily care.

ORIGINALLY BRED to hunt elk, lynx, wolves and small game.

Special characteristics
The Elkhound is playful, active and inquisitive.

Exercise requirements
High. Very active and needs plenty of exercise.

Attitude to
OWNERS independent, loyal
CHILDREN good
OTHER PETS may be problematic with small pets
STRANGERS reserved, need to be socialized well
UNFAMILIAR DOGS can be difficult with dogs they live with

Perfect owner
Active, easy-going owner with tolerant neighbours who likes the Elkhound's independent, extrovert nature and who can provide plenty of exercise and grooming.

Potential problems
May bark excessively. Lack of exercise may lead to digging or escaping.

The Elkhound's bushy tail is tightly curled over the back.

⚠️ This dog sheds loose hair in the house, and will need daily grooming.

Hounds

Finnish Spitz

alert • lively • friendly • independent • eager • courageous • strong-willed

SIZE 39–50 cm (15½–20 in) • WEIGHT 14–16 kg (31–35 lb) • COAT Thick, short to medium length
• COLOUR Reddish-brown or gold • LIFESPAN 13 years • In the 'Non-Sporting' class in the USA

Hounds

Clean and cat-like, the Finnish Spitz is an eager, energetic, independent companion for vigorous walks. Active and curious, they are alert and very vocal and make good watchdogs.

ORIGINALLY BRED for flushing birds, squirrels and martens into trees then barking continually while waiting for the hunter.

Special characteristics
The Finnish Spitz is active and curious, with a tendency to bark.

Exercise requirements
High. Needs energetic walks.

Attitude to
OWNERS independent, wilful
CHILDREN good
OTHER PETS may be problematic with small pets
STRANGERS reserved, good watchdog
UNFAMILIAR DOGS friendly

Perfect owner
Active, easy-going owner who has tolerant neighbours and who will enjoy vigorous walks with their energetic, independent pet.

Potential problems
May bark excessively. Owners need to discourage this during puppyhood.

⚠ The thick coat will need daily grooming to keep it in good condition, but these dogs like to keep themselves clean.

Foxhound (English)

stamina • endurance • strong desire to hunt • friendly

SIZE **53–69 cm (21–27 in)** • WEIGHT **25–34 kg (55–75 lb)** • COAT **Short and dense** • COLOUR **Any recognized hound colour and markings** • LIFESPAN **11 years**

Bred to hunt in packs, foxhounds are happiest with constant company. Large and eager, they investigate everything and anything, often at the expense of household furnishings. Their energy and stamina is more than the average pet owner needs and wants and exercising these active, independent hunters can be difficult. American Foxhounds are taller and lighter-boned than English Foxhounds.

ORIGINALLY BRED to hunt foxes in a pack with huntsmen on horseback.

Perfect owner
Owner with facilities and land to keep a working pack, or very tolerant, non-house-proud, active, energetic pet owner with access to safe places to exercise.

Potential problems
Tends to run off on walks, escape from the garden or yard, and may be destructive if bored or under-exercised. May be problematic if left alone at home.

Special characteristics
Active and very inquisitive, the Foxhound is also interested in scents.

Exercise requirements
High. Needs a great deal of exercise to burn off energy.

Attitude to
OWNERS **independent, affectionate**
CHILDREN **good**
OTHER PETS **may kill small pets, may chase**
STRANGERS **friendly**
UNFAMILIAR DOGS **friendly**

Hounds

Grand Bleu de Gasgogne

gentle • active • kind • methodical • determined • confident

SIZE 60–70 cm (23½–27½ in) • WEIGHT 32–35 kg (71–77 lb) • COAT Smooth, short • COLOUR Black marked on a white base, but covered entirely with black mottling, which gives a blue appearance • LIFESPAN 12–14 years

Hounds

Grand Bleu de Gasgognes are large and powerful, but gentle and friendly. With enough stamina to keep running all day, long walks in safe areas are essential. At home, these independent hounds are calm, affectionate and placid.

ORIGINALLY BRED to trail wolves, wild boar and deer for hunters.

Special characteristics
This active dog is very interested in scents.

Exercise requirements
High. Needs plenty of exercise outdoors, calm at home.

Attitude to
OWNERS independent, affectionate
CHILDREN good
OTHER PETS good, may chase
STRANGERS friendly, can be reserved
UNFAMILIAR DOGS friendly

Perfect owner
Active, easy-going owner who enjoys long walks with a large dog that is interested in scent trails.

Potential problems
May be difficult to control on walks.

Greyhound

calm • gentle • affectionate • even-tempered

SIZE **69–76 cm (27–30 in)** • WEIGHT **27–32 kg (60–70 lb)** • COAT **Fine and close** • COLOUR **Black, white, red, blue, fawn, fallow, brindle or any of these colours broken with white** • LIFESPAN **11–12 years**

The fastest animal on earth apart from the cheetah, greyhounds run in short bursts of breakneck speed. At home, these gentle, affectionate pets are happy to lie around all day, but prefer the sofa to the floor, where they can be more comfortable.

ORIGINALLY BRED for coursing hares.

Special characteristics
The Greyhound loves to chase, and is fast enough to catch most animals.

Exercise requirements
Medium. Needs off-lead running.

Attitude to
OWNERS independent, affectionate
CHILDREN good, tolerant
OTHER PETS may be problematic with small pets, may chase and injure cats unless raised with them
STRANGERS friendly
UNFAMILIAR DOGS friendly, may chase small dogs

Perfect owner
Gentle, easy-going owner who enjoys frequent short energetic walks and who lives near to safe, open areas where these elegant dogs can run free.

Potential problems
May be difficult to control on walks. Most greyhounds will chase if given the chance and may kill small animals if they catch them.

Hounds

Basset Griffon Vendeen (Petit & Grand)

happy • extrovert • bold • independent • willing to please

SIZE Petit: 33–38 cm (13–15 in) • Grand: 38–42 cm (15–16 in) • WEIGHT Petit: 14–18 kg (31–40 lb) • Grand: 18–20 kg (40–44 lb) • COAT Rough, long, harsh with thick undercoat • COLOUR White with any combination of lemon, orange, tricolour or grizzle markings • LIFESPAN 12 years

Hounds

The good-natured, extrovert Basset Griffon Vendeen is friendly and willing to please. Walks can quickly turn into a hunt unless exercise is restricted to lead-walking or safe areas.

ORIGINALLY BRED to flush out rabbits and hares.

Special characteristics
Very active, this hound has a special interest in scents.

Exercise requirements
High. Enjoys long walks.

Attitude to
OWNERS affectionate, independent streak
CHILDREN good
OTHER PETS good
STRANGERS friendly
UNFAMILIAR DOGS friendly

Perfect owner
Active, easy-going owner who enjoys plenty of energetic walks.

Potential problems
May be difficult to control on walks. Barking may be a problem. Lack of exercise may result in digging and other behaviour problems.

⚠ The dog's coat will bring in mud and dirt from outside.

Hamiltonstövare

gentle • even-tempered • happy • exuberant • extrovert • strong-willed

SIZE 46–60 cm (18–23½ in) • WEIGHT 23–27 kg (50–60 lb) • COAT Smooth, short • COLOUR Black and brown with white markings • LIFESPAN 12–13 years

Bred from foxhounds and harriers, the Hamiltonstövare was originally called the Swedish Foxhound. Easy-going and friendly at home, these dogs quickly turn into determined hunters outside that will efficiently follow a scent or chase prey to the exclusion of all else.

ORIGINALLY BRED for hunting hares and foxes, finding and flushing game.

Special characteristics

Active and interested in scents, the Hamiltonstövare also has a strong desire to hunt.

Exercise requirements

High. Active and energetic outside, lazy indoors.

Attitude to

OWNERS independent, affectionate
CHILDREN good, tolerant
OTHER PETS may be problematic with small pets
STRANGERS friendly
UNFAMILIAR DOGS friendly

Perfect owner

Easy-going owner who is able to provide plenty of exercise for this active, energetic dog.

Potential problems

A strong desire to hunt may make it difficult to find safe places to exercise this dog. Lack of exercise may lead to destructiveness and other behaviour problems.

Hounds

Harrier

active • independent • gregarious

SIZE **46–56 cm (18–22 in)** • WEIGHT **22–27 kg (48–60 lb)** • COAT **Smooth, short** • COLOUR **Any**
• LIFESPAN **10–12 years**

Hounds

Bred to hunt in a pack, Harriers love company and are affectionate and friendly. They have tremendous energy and a strong desire to hunt and for this reason are less than ideal pets unless owners have the facilities to exercise them safely.

ORIGINALLY BRED to hunt hares in a pack with hunters on foot.

Attitude to
OWNERS **independent, affectionate**
CHILDREN **good**
OTHER PETS **may be problematic with small pets**
STRANGERS **friendly**
UNFAMILIAR DOGS **friendly**

Perfect owner
Owner who has facilities and enough land to keep a working pack, or experienced, easy-going owner who will run or bike with their Harrier every day and will appreciate their independent nature.

Potential problems
May be difficult to control on walks. Lack of exercise may lead to destructiveness and other behaviour problems. May be problematic if left alone at home.

Special characteristics
The active Harrier has a strong desire to hunt, and is interested in scents.

Exercise requirements
High. Needs plenty of space to run off abundant energy.

Ibizan Hound

reserved • dignified • independent • alert • affectionate

SIZE **56–74 cm (22–29 in)** • WEIGHT **19–25 kg (42–55 lb)** • COAT **Smooth, close, dense. Can also be wiry or long** • COLOUR **White, chestnut or lion solid colour, or any combination of these** • LIFESPAN **12 years**

Sensitive, gentle and loyal, Ibizan Hounds make elegant, independent pets. They are built for speed so large and safe exercise areas are essential for these alert, enthusiastic chasers.

ORIGINALLY BRED to course rabbits and hares.

Special characteristics
This hound likes to run fast, jump and chase.

Exercise requirements
High. Needs to run outside, but lazy at home.

Attitude to
OWNERS **independent, affectionate**
CHILDREN **good, tolerant**
OTHER PETS **may be problematic with small pets unless raised with them**
STRANGERS **reserved**
UNFAMILIAR DOGS **friendly**

Perfect owner
Easy-going owner who can offer frequent walks to a safe place for off-lead running and who will enjoy their gentle, independent spirit.

Potential problems
May be difficult to control on walks.

Hounds

Irish Wolfhound

gentle • kind • friendly • calm • patient

SIZE **71–80 cm (28–31 in)** • WEIGHT **41–55 kg (90–120 lb)** • COAT **Rough and harsh** • COLOUR **Grey, brindle, red, black, pure white, fawn, wheaten and steel grey** • LIFESPAN **8–10 years**

Hounds

These gentle giants are calm, affectionate and friendly. Once bred by royalty to hunt wolves, they are fast runners outside and need fast runs in a safe area. At home they are relaxed and independent.

ORIGINALLY BRED to hunt wolves in packs.

Special characteristics
The Irish Wolfhound likes to run fast for short periods, and to chase.

Exercise requirements
Medium. Content to be lazy when at home.

Attitude to
OWNERS independent, affectionate
CHILDREN good, may knock over young children
OTHER PETS may be problematic with small pets
STRANGERS friendly
UNFAMILIAR DOGS friendly

Perfect owner
Strong, easy-going, affectionate owner who has enough space to accommodate this giant and who can provide a safe area for daily off-lead running.

Potential problems
May be difficult to control on walks if they see something to chase.

Lurcher

gentle • affectionate • even-tempered

SIZE **51–61 cm (20–24 in)** • WEIGHT **12.5–14.5 kg (27½–32 lb)** • COAT **Wiry or smooth** • COLOUR **Any**
• LIFESPAN **14 years**

Bred originally for harecoursing, Lurchers have a combination of the speed of the greyhound with the reactivity of the collie. They are gentle, affectionate and independent at home, but quickly move in for the chase when out on a walk.

ORIGINALLY BRED for coursing hares.

Special characteristics
Fast enough to catch most animals, the Lurcher loves to chase.

Exercise requirements
Medium. Needs off-lead running.

Attitude to
OWNERS **independent, affectionate**
CHILDREN **good, tolerant**
OTHER PETS **may be problematic with small pets, may chase and injure cats unless raised with them**
STRANGERS **friendly**
UNFAMILIAR DOGS **friendly, may chase small dogs**

Perfect owner
Gentle, easy-going owner who enjoys frequent energetic walks and who lives near to safe, open areas where these elegant dogs can run free.

Potential problems
May be difficult to control on walks. Most lurchers will chase if given the chance and may kill small animals if they catch them.

Hounds

Norwegian Lundehund

agile • alert • energetic • lively • responsive

SIZE **32–38 cm (12½–15 in)** • WEIGHT **6–7 kg (13–15½ lb)** • COAT Dense, rough outer coat with soft undercoat • COLOUR Reddish-brown to fallow with black tips to hairs preferred. Black or grey. All with white markings. White with dark markings • LIFESPAN **12 years**

Bred to collect puffins from cliff nests, these unusual dogs have extra toes to help give a better grip on the rocks. They are also more agile than most with a very flexible neck, and are lively, affectionate and playful.

ORIGINALLY BRED in northen Norway to collect puffins from nests on cliffs.

Exercise requirements
Medium. Enjoys playing.

Attitude to
OWNERS **affectionate**
CHILDREN **good, playful**
OTHER PETS **good**
STRANGERS **friendly**
UNFAMILIAR DOGS **friendly**

Perfect owner
Active, easy-going affectionate owner who likes to play with their dog.

Potential problems
May be difficult to housetrain.

Special characteristics
This playful dog has at least six toes on each foot with big pads and double dewclaws to give it better grip.

Otterhound

amiable • cheerful • affectionate • independent • even-tempered

SIZE 61–69 cm (24–27 in) • WEIGHT 30–55 kg (65–120 lb) • COAT Long, dense, rough, harsh
• COLOUR Any hound colour • LIFESPAN 12 years

These happy, shaggy dogs are good swimmers and have a coat that keeps out the cold. Otterhounds are good-natured and amiable, but following scents and hunting are high on the list of things they like to do best.

ORIGINALLY BRED to hunt otters.

Attitude to
OWNERS independent, affectionate
CHILDREN good, tolerant
OTHER PETS may be problematic with small pets
STRANGERS friendly
UNFAMILIAR DOGS friendly

Perfect owner
Active, easy-going, affectionate owner who is able to provide safe places for this dog to run and swim.

Potential problems
May be difficult to control on walks.

Special characteristics
Active and interested in scents, the Otterhound is happy to completely submerge in water.

Exercise requirements
High. Enjoys running and swimming

Hounds

Pharaoh Hound

alert • aloof • friendly • affectionate

SIZE 53–63 cm (21–25 in) • WEIGHT 20–25 kg (45–55 lb) • COAT Short and glossy • COLOUR Tan or rich tan • LIFESPAN 12–14 years

Hounds

Sensitive and gentle, the Pharaoh Hound has origins that can be traced back to the Ancient Egyptians. Their hunting and chasing instincts are still strong so care is needed on walks. Aloof and independent, they will be affectionate and friendly but on their own terms.

ORIGINALLY BRED for hunting using sight, sound and smell.

Special characteristics
This dog has a curious nature. It is a keen, energetic hunter, and will blush when excited.

Exercise requirements
Very high. Needs to run and chase.

Attitude to
OWNERS independent, affectionate
CHILDREN good
OTHER PETS may be problematic with small pets
STRANGERS reserved but friendly
UNFAMILIAR DOGS friendly

Perfect owner
Active easy-going owner who has time and access to safe places to exercise this energetic, independent dog daily.

Potential problems
May be difficult to control on walks. Some dogs bark excessively.

Plott Hound

affectionate • independent • easy-going • energetic

SIZE 51–61 cm (20–24 in) • WEIGHT 20–25 kg (45–55 lb) • COAT Short and glossy • COLOUR Brindle or blue
• LIFESPAN 12–13 years • In 'Miscellaneous' class in the USA

Plott Hounds are strong, vigorous hunters. Affectionate, friendly and easy-going at home, they are very active and need plenty of free running exercise in safe areas to keep them happy.

ORIGINALLY BRED to 'tree' bear and raccoons until the hunters arrived.

Special characteristics
This very active hound is interested in scents and hunting.

Exercise requirements
High. Loves to run freely, quieter at home.

Attitude to
OWNERS independent, affectionate
CHILDREN good
OTHER PETS may be problematic with small pets
STRANGERS friendly
UNFAMILIAR DOGS friendly

Perfect owner
Active, easy-going owner who enjoys energetic walks in areas where this independent hunter can run loose safely.

Potential problems
May be difficult to control on walks, and can be noisy.

Hounds

Rhodesian Ridgeback

dignified • aloof • strong-willed • loyal • confident

SIZE 61–69 cm (24–27 in) • WEIGHT 30–39 kg (65–85 lb) • COAT Short and dense • COLOUR Light wheaten to red wheaten • LIFESPAN 12 years

Hounds

Rhodesian Ridgebacks are strong and courageous and like to chase. They have a discerning, independent character and are prone to ignoring owners' requests unless they see a reason for compliance.

ORIGINALLY BRED in Africa to track lions and hold them at bay while hunters arrived.

Attitude to
OWNERS independent, affectionate
CHILDREN good
OTHER PETS may be problematic with small pets, will chase cats unless raised with them
STRANGERS discerning, intuitive
UNFAMILIAR DOGS good if well socialized

Perfect owner
Experienced, strong-willed, active owner who has safe places to walk this independent, powerful hunter.

Potential problems
May be difficult to control on walks. If badly bred or raised incorrectly, some dogs may be aggressive.

Special characteristics
The Rhodesian Ridgeback is a powerful dog that likes to chase. It has a distinctive ridge of hair on its back that gives it its name.

Exercise requirements
High. Lazy at home.

Saluki

dignified • sensitive • gentle • independent

SIZE **58–71 cm (23–28 in)** • WEIGHT **14–25 kg (31–55 lb)** • COAT **Smooth, soft silky texture**
• COLOUR **Any other than brindle** • LIFESPAN **12 years**

Elegant, gentle, sensitive Salukis are aloof and independent by nature. They are very fast runners and care is needed to exercise them in places where they can use up their energy, but where they cannot chase other animals.

ORIGINALLY BRED **to hunt gazelle.**

Special characteristics
The Saluki is a fast runner and loves to chase.

Exercise requirements
High. Enjoys long runs, but quiet at home.

Attitude to
OWNERS **independent, not tactile**
CHILDREN **will tolerate, but may dislike young children**
OTHER PETS **may be problematic with small pets**
STRANGERS **reserved**
UNFAMILIAR DOGS **reserved but friendly**

Perfect owner
Active, easy-going owner who can find safe places for this active breed to run free and who will enjoy their independent, aloof nature.

Potential problems
Will chase anything that looks like prey.

Hounds

Segugio Italiano

gentle • affectionate • even-tempered

SIZE 48–59 cm (19–23 in) • WEIGHT 18–28 kg (40–62 lb) • COAT Shorthaired: Smooth, thick, shiny • Coarsehaired: Harsh, dense, wiry • COLOUR Black/tan or any shade from deep red to wheaten • LIFESPAN 12–13 years

Hounds

A popular hunting dog in Italy, the Segugio Italiano is friendly and easy-going with people. Independent but affectionate, these dogs need long, active walks to use up their high energy reserves.

ORIGINALLY BRED to hunt large game by sight and scent.

Special characteristics
This active dog is very interested in scents.

Exercise requirements
High. Enjoys long walks.

Attitude to
OWNERS independent, affectionate
CHILDREN good
OTHER PETS can be problematic with small pets
STRANGERS friendly
UNFAMILIAR DOGS friendly

Perfect owner
Active, easy-going owner who has access to safe areas to exercise this energetic, independent hunter.

Potential problems
May be difficult to control on walks.

Sloughi

quiet • alert • dignified • haughty • aloof • sensitive • loyal

SIZE 61–72 cm (24–28 in) • WEIGHT 20–27 kg (45–60 lb) • COAT Fine and short • COLOUR Light sand to red sand • LIFESPAN 12 years

Fast-moving Sloughis have strong hunting instincts and are built to run at speed after prey. Aloof and sometimes shy, they prefer their owners to strangers. Quiet at home, they need long, vigorous, energetic walks to keep them well exercised.

ORIGINALLY BRED for hunting desert animals such as gazelles.

Attitude to
OWNERS independent, affectionate
CHILDREN can be difficult
OTHER PETS may be problematic with small pets
STRANGERS reserved, territorial
UNFAMILIAR DOGS tolerates

Perfect owner
Experienced, gentle owner who leads a quiet life and has access to places to exercise this energetic hunter.

Potential problems
May display control problems on walks and territorial or nervous aggression towards people. May prey on small pets.

Special characteristics
The Sloughi has strong hunting instincts and a timid, sensitive nature.

Exercise requirements
High. Content to be lazy at home.

Hounds

Whippet

gentle • affectionate • even disposition

SIZE **44–51 cm (17½–20 in)** • WEIGHT **12.5–13.5 kg (27–30 lb)** • COAT **Fine, short** • COLOUR **Any**
• LIFESPAN **13–14 years**

Hounds

Sweet-natured and affectionate with owners, Whippets can sometimes be shy and timid with strangers. Nicknamed 'the poor man's racehorse', they are perfectly built for speed so they need safe exercise areas.

ORIGINALLY BRED to chase and kill rabbits.

Special characteristics
The whippet is a fast runner, especially interested in hunting.

Exercise requirements
Medium. Needs to run free, but lazy at home.

Attitude to
OWNERS **independent, affectionate**
CHILDREN **good,**
OTHER PETS **problematic with small pets**
STRANGERS **reserved, then friendly**
UNFAMILIAR DOGS **friendly**

Perfect owner
Gentle, easy-going active owner who has safe places to allow free running of this small, independent hunter.

Potential problems
May be difficult to control on walks.

 This dog has a fine coat and may feel the cold. It prefers soft bedding.

Anatolian Shepherd Dog

strong-willed • bold • independent • proud • confident

SIZE 71–81 cm (28–32 in) • WEIGHT 41–64 kg (90–141 lb) • COAT Short, dense with thick undercoat
• COLOUR Cream to fawn, with black mask and ears • LIFESPAN 10–11 years • In 'Working' class in the USA

Bred to guard, Anatolian Shepherd Dogs are a force to be reckoned with. Strongly built, they have a strong nature and are bold and independent, requiring a great deal of socialization to ensure they are pleasant to visitors and other dogs.

ORIGINALLY BRED to guard sheep from wolves and bears.

Special characteristics
This dog is naturally suspicious.

Exercise requirements
Low. Needs plenty of mental stimulation.

Attitude to
OWNERS: loyal, affectionate
CHILDREN: natural guard
OTHER PETS: accepted
STRANGERS: suspicious, territorial
UNFAMILIAR DOGS: not tolerant of others

Perfect owner
Experienced, strong-willed, physically strong owner with a secure garden or yard who is willing to give this powerful dog a job to do to keep its lively mind occupied.

Potential problems
May be aggressive to strangers and unfamiliar dogs. May display status-related aggression towards gentle owners.

Pastoral

Australian Cattle Dog

loyal • protective • amenable • biddable • alert • courageous

SIZE **43–51 cm (17–20 in)** • WEIGHT **16–20 kg (35–45 lb)** • COAT **Smooth, straight, hard topcoat with short dense undercoat** • COLOUR **Blue, red speckle** • LIFESPAN **12 years**

Pastoral

Reactive and responsive, but robust and courageous, Australian Cattle Dogs are strong-willed and tough. They are very active dogs and need a job to pour their energies into.

ORIGINALLY BRED for cattle herding.

Special characteristics
This playful dog has great strength of character. It is particularly suspicious of strangers.

Exercise requirements
Very high. Needs a great deal of stimulation and play.

Attitude to
OWNERS affectionate, loyal
CHILDREN tolerant, but not of their friends unless well socialized
OTHER PETS alright if raised with them
STRANGERS suspicious, territorial
UNFAMILIAR DOGS can be problematic unless well socialized

Perfect owner
Experienced, strong-willed, considerate owner who has enough time and energy to give this powerful dog a job to do and an outlet for its strong drives through play and training.

Potential problems
May be aggressive to strangers and other animals unless properly socialized. May display status-related aggression to gentle owners, and may nip at heels in play.

Australian Shepherd

responsive • loyal • attentive • enthusiastic • reserved • biddable

SIZE **46–58 cm (18–23 in)** • WEIGHT **16–32 kg (35–70 lb)** • COAT **Medium wavy with undercoat** • COLOUR **Blue merle, black, red merle, red, all with or without tan points** • LIFESPAN **12–13 years**

Virtually unknown in Australia, the Australian Shepherd was develop exclusively in the USA, being useful on farms and ranches. The resulting dog has strong herding and guarding instincts and a high energy level.

ORIGINALLY BRED **to herd sheep.**

Attitude to

OWNERS **loyal, affectionate**
CHILDREN **protective**
OTHER PETS **good, may chase**
STRANGERS **reserved, territorial**
UNFAMILIAR DOGS **tolerant**

Perfect owner
Experienced, strong-willed, considerate owner who has enough time and energy to give this active dog a job and an outlet for its strong drives through play and training.

Potential problems
Some dogs may display chasing problems. May be aggressive towards strangers if they are inadequately socialized.

Special characteristics
This dog has strong herding and guarding instincts.

Exercise requirements
High. Full of energy.

Pastoral

Bearded Collie

alert • lively • exuberant • confident • active

SIZE 51–56 cm (20–22 in) • WEIGHT 18–27 kg (40–60 lb) • COAT Outer coat flat, harsh, strong and shaggy with soft, furry undercoat • COLOUR Slate-grey, reddish-fawn, black, blue, all shades of grey, brown and sandy with or without white markings • LIFESPAN 12–13 years

Pastoral

Bearded Collies are lively, exuberant and full of energy, but can be exercised easily as they are playful by nature. Close bonding and responsive, they need daily care to keep their coats in good condition.

ORIGINALLY BRED to herd sheep.

Special characteristics
This collie is lively and playful, and enjoys chasing.

Exercise requirements
High. Needs to run and play.

Attitude to
OWNERS affectionate, biddable
CHILDREN good
OTHER PETS good, will chase
STRANGERS friendly, can be reserved
UNFAMILIAR DOGS friendly

Perfect owner
Gentle, active owner who has enough time and energy to play, exercise and train this exuberant, energetic, playful dog.

Potential problems
May display chase problems if not directed onto toys. May be possessive over toys. Sound sensitive and prone to developing noise phobias.

⚠ The coat needs daily attention to keep it in good condition, and the hair should be tied up out of their eyes so that they can see clearly.

Belgian Shepherd Dogs

Belgian Shepherd Dogs come in four different coat varieties. They have a reactive, retiring nature and, as a result, can be timid and easily frightened. They are energetic, active dogs that need an outlet for their strong desire to chase, and are responsive and like to form close attachments to their owners.

Malinois

wary • active • alert • biddable • protective • resourceful

SIZE 56–66 cm (22–26 in) • WEIGHT 27.5–28.5 kg (61–63 lb) • COAT Short with woolly undercoat • COLOUR All shades of red, fawn, grey with black overlay. Black mask on face • LIFESPAN 12–13 years

ORIGINALLY BRED to herd livestock.

Special characteristics
This active and playful dog likes to chase.

Exercise requirements
High. Needs both physical exercise and mental stimulation.

Attitude to
OWNERS loyal, affectionate
CHILDREN good if well socialized
OTHER PETS good, may chase
STRANGERS wary, territorial
UNFAMILIAR DOGS good if well socialized

Perfect owner
Experienced, considerate owner who will take care with this shy breed and provide plenty of exercise, games and training to use up their boundless mental and physical energy.

Potential problems
May be aggressive to strangers. Chasing instincts may cause a problem.

Pastoral

Groenendael

wary • active • alert • biddable • protective • resourceful

SIZE **56–66 cm (22–26 in)** • WEIGHT **27.5–28.5 kg (61–63 lb)** • COAT **Outer coat long, straight and abundant with very dense undercoat** • COLOUR **Black** • LIFESPAN **12–13 years**

Pastoral

ORIGINALLY BRED **to herd livestock.**

Special characteristics
This active and playful dog likes to chase.

Exercise requirements
High. Needs both physical exercise and mental stimulation.

Attitude to
OWNERS **loyal, affectionate**
CHILDREN **good if well socialized**
OTHER PETS **good, may chase**
STRANGERS **wary, territorial**
UNFAMILIAR DOGS **good if well socialized**

Perfect owner
Experienced, considerate owner who will take care with this shy breed and provide plenty of exercise, games and training to use up their boundless mental and physical energy.

Potential problems
May be aggressive to strangers. Chasing instincts may cause a problem.

Laekenois

wary • active • alert • biddable • protective • resourceful

SIZE **56–66 cm (22–26 in)** • WEIGHT **27.5–28.5 kg (61–63 lb)** • COAT **Harsh, wiry, dry and not curly**
• COLOUR **Reddish-fawn with black shading** • LIFESPAN **12–13 years**

ORIGINALLY BRED to herd livestock.

Special characteristics
This active and playful dog likes to chase.

Exercise requirements
High. Needs both physical exercise and mental stimulation.

Attitude to
OWNERS loyal, affectionate
CHILDREN good if well socialized
OTHER PETS good, may chase
STRANGERS wary, territorial
UNFAMILIAR DOGS good if well socialized

Perfect owner
Experienced, considerate owner who will take care with this shy breed and provide plenty of exercise, games and training to use up their boundless mental and physical energy.

Potential problems
May be aggressive to strangers, although less likely than in the other Belgian Shepherds. Chasing instincts may cause problems.

Pastoral

Tervueren

wary • active • alert • biddable • protective • resourceful

SIZE **56–66 cm (22–26 in)** • WEIGHT **27.5–28.5 kg (61–63 lb)** • COAT Outer coat long, straight and abundant with very dense undercoat. Hair especially long and abundant, ruff-like around neck, particularly in males. Fringe of long hair down back of forelegs, on hindquarters and tail • COLOUR All shades of red, fawn, grey with black overlay. Black mask on face. Tail should have a darker or black tip • LIFESPAN **12–13 years**

Pastoral

ORIGINALLY BRED to herd livestock.

Special characteristics
This active and playful dog likes to chase.

Exercise requirements
High. Needs both physical exercise and mental stimulation.

Attitude to
OWNERS loyal, affectionate
CHILDREN good if well socialized
OTHER PETS good, may chase
STRANGERS wary, territorial
UNFAMILIAR DOGS good if well socialized

Perfect owner
Experienced, considerate owner who will take care with this shy breed and provide plenty of exercise, games and training to use up their boundless mental and physical energy.

Potential problems
May be aggressive to strangers. Chasing instincts may cause a problem.

Bergamasco

vigilant • strongly protective • cautious • patient

SIZE **54–62 cm (21–24½ in)** • WEIGHT **26–38 kg (56–84 lb)** • COAT Abundant and long with short, dense undercoat. Tends to form into strands or loose mats. Greasy to the touch • COLOUR Black, various shades of grey • LIFESPAN **12 years**

Relatively rare, Bergamascos are an ancient, hardy breed that originated in the Iranian mountains where they were bred to tend and guard sheep. Resilient and vigorous, Bergamascos are independent and protective.

ORIGINALLY BRED to guard flocks of sheep from wolves.

Special characteristics
This dog has a strong desire to guard.

Perfect owner
Experienced, strong-willed owner with a secure garden or yard who is willing to find activities to keep its lively mind occupied.

Potential problems
This dog may display aggression towards strangers.

⚠ Pet dogs may be more comfortable and less smelly if shaved, especially if living indoors. Hair needs to be pulled back or shaved around the eyes so they can see clearly.

Exercise requirements
Low. Needs mental stimulation.

Attitude to
OWNERS loyal, affectionate
CHILDREN good, but may not be with visiting children
OTHER PETS good if raised with them
STRANGERS suspicious, territorial
UNFAMILIAR DOGS can be problematic

Pastoral

Border Collie

tenacious • keen • biddable • alert • responsive • sensitive

SIZE **46–54 cm (18–21 in)** • WEIGHT **14–22 kg (30–49 lb)** • COAT **Medium length, abundant, smooth with soft, dense undercoat** • COLOUR **Variety of colours permissible. White should never predominate** • LIFESPAN **12–14 years**

Quick, alert and reactive, Border Collies are well known around the world. They have strong desire to chase from an early age, which needs to be channelled into acceptable outlets such as games with toys. They form close bonds with owners and have abundant energy and stamina.

ORIGINALLY BRED **to herd sheep.**

Special characteristics
The Border Collie has plenty of stamina, and likes to chase.

Exercise requirements
Very high. Needs exercise and plenty of games.

Attitude to
OWNERS **devoted, affectionate**
CHILDREN **good, may chase/nip in play**
OTHER PETS **good, may chase**
STRANGERS **good if well socialized**
UNFAMILIAR DOGS **good if well socialized**

Perfect owner
Energetic, loving families who have enough time to find this dog a job to do, and enough energy to exercise, train and channel this dog's strong chase drives into games and play.

Potential problems
May display chase problems, and aggression to strangers if not well socialized. Some dogs may have noise phobias.

⚠️ The dog's coat will bring in mud and dirt from outside.

Briard

versatile • bold • calm • courageous • biddable

SIZE **58–69 cm (23–27 in)** • WEIGHT **33.5–34.5 kg (74–76 lb)** • COAT **Long, slightly wavy and dry with a fine dense undercoat** • COLOUR **Black, fawn, slate grey** • LIFESPAN **12 years**

Strong-natured Briards were bred to be sheep herders and guarders so they are active and like to chase. They need plenty of socialization to prevent their suspicious nature getting the better of them, but are calm and courteous if raised well.

ORIGINALLY BRED for herding and guarding livestock.

Special characteristics
The Briard is an active and protective dog.

Exercise requirements
Medium. Needs plenty of games.

Attitude to
OWNERS affectionate, protective
CHILDREN good if raised with them
OTHER PETS good if raised with them
STRANGERS friendly if well socialized
UNFAMILIAR DOGS friendly if well socialized, can be bossy

Perfect owner
Experienced, strong-willed, active owner who can provide this responsive dog with a job to do as well as plenty of games, activity and socialization.

Potential problems
May be aggressive to strangers and other dogs if not well socialized.

Pastoral

⚠️ The long hair over this dog's eyes needs to be cut or tied back so it can see clearly.

Collie (Rough)

sensitive • aloof • affectionate • gentle

SIZE 51–61 cm (20–24 in) • WEIGHT 18–30 kg (40–66 lb) • COAT Outer coat long, profuse, straight and harsh to touch, with soft, furry undercoat • COLOUR Sable and white, tricolour, blue merle with white collar, full or part, white shirt, legs and feet, white tail tip • LIFESPAN 12–13 years

Pastoral

Sensitive and aloof, the Rough Collie is well known thanks to the 'Lassie' films. Gentle, affectionate and responsive to owners, this heavily coated breed is quite difficult to socialize well and tends to be reserved with strangers and concerned about anything new.

ORIGINALLY BRED to herd sheep.

Special characteristics
This playful collie likes to chase.

Exercise requirements
Low.

Attitude to
OWNERS loyal, affectionate
CHILDREN will tolerate
OTHER PETS good
STRANGERS reserved
UNFAMILIAR DOGS reserved or indifferent

Perfect owner
Gentle, sensitive owner who will enjoy the daily grooming sessions and the close bond.

Potential problems
May be wary of strangers, and some dogs may have noise phobias.

⚠ Daily coat care is required to ensure this breed remains tangle-free. Its profuse coat can lead to overheating in summer, when special care must be taken to keep it cool.

Collie (Smooth)

sensitive • aloof • affectionate • gentle

SIZE 51–61 cm (20–24 in) • WEIGHT 18–30 kg (40–66 lb) • COAT Short, flat, topcoat of harsh texture, with very dense undercoat • COLOUR Sable and white, tricolour, blue merle with white collar, full or part, white shirt, legs and feet, white tail tip • LIFESPAN 12–13 years

Sensitive and aloof, the Smooth Collie is gentle, affectionate and responsive to owners. This breed can be difficult to socialize well and tends to be reserved with strangers and concerned about anything new.

ORIGINALLY BRED to herd sheep.

Special characteristics
This collie is playful and likes to chase.

Exercise requirements
Low.

Attitude to
OWNERS loyal, affectionate
CHILDREN will tolerate
OTHER PETS good
STRANGERS shy
UNFAMILIAR DOGS reserved or indifferent

Perfect owner
Gentle, sensitive owner who will enjoy the close bond and protect these shy dogs from frightening experiences.

Potential problems
May be snappy with strangers, and suffer from noise phobias.

Pastoral

Estrela Mountain Dog

active • loyal • affectionate • alert • strong-willed • stubborn

SIZE **62–72 cm (24½–28½ in)** • WEIGHT **30–50 kg (66–110 lb)** • COAT **Long coat: Thick, moderately harsh outer coat, with very dense, paler undercoat.** • **Short coat: Short, thick, moderately harsh and straight, with shorter dense undercoat** • COLOUR **Fawn, brindle, wolf with black muzzle or mask** • LIFESPAN **10–12 years**

Pastoral

Powerful and sturdy, Estrela Mountain Dogs are loyal and alert with a strong guarding instinct. They are independent and can be stubborn too, and need strong-willed, experienced owners.

ORIGINALLY BRED to guard flocks of sheep from wolves.

Special characteristics
This strong-willed dog has a powerful guarding instinct.

Exercise requirements
Low.

Attitude to
OWNERS **loyal, affectionate**
CHILDREN **natural guard**
OTHER PETS **accepted**
STRANGERS **suspicious, territorial**
UNFAMILIAR DOGS **not tolerant of others**

Perfect owner
Experienced, strong-willed, physically strong owner with a secure garden or yard who is willing to give this powerful dog a job to do to keep its lively mind occupied.

Potential problems
Tendency to be aggressive to strangers and unfamiliar dogs. May display status-related aggression towards gentle owners.

Finnish Lapphund

responsive • brave • calm • faithful • cooperative

SIZE 41–52 cm (16–20½ in) • WEIGHT 20–21 kg (44–47 lb) • COAT Profuse, long, coarse outer coat with soft, thick undercoat • COLOUR All colours are allowed, but the main colour must dominate • LIFESPAN 11–12 years

The thickly coated Finnish Lapphund was bred for life in cold countries and can get uncomfortably hot in summer. Playful, with a desire to chase, they are loyal and cooperative with owners.

ORIGINALLY BRED to herd reindeer.

Special characteristics
This playful dog has a strong desire to chase.

Exercise requirements
Medium. Loves to play.

Attitude to
OWNERS loyal, affectionate
CHILDREN good
OTHER PETS good, may chase
STRANGERS good if well socialized
UNFAMILIAR DOGS good if well socialized

Perfect owner
Easy-going owner who has the time to train and play with a dog that loves to chase.

Potential problems
May chase things it should not.

⚠ This dog requires regular grooming to keep its thick coat free from mats.

Pastoral

German Shepherd Dog (Alsatian)

attentive • alert • steady • loyal • self-assured • sensitive • responsive

SIZE **58–63 cm (23–25 in)** • WEIGHT **34–43 kg (75–95 lb)** • COAT **Straight, hard outer coat of medium to long length with thick undercoat** • COLOUR **Black or black saddle with tan or gold to light grey markings. All black, all grey, with lighter or brown markings** • LIFESPAN **12–13 years**

Pastoral

The ubiquitous German Shepherd Dog is a versatile breed, chosen to be police dogs, guide dogs and guard dogs around the world. Loyal and protective, these dogs are alert, reactive and have abundant energy, but need early socialization to prevent them being wary of strangers and other dogs.

ORIGINALLY BRED to herd sheep.

Special characteristics
This active and powerful dog has a strong desire to chase.

Exercise requirements
High. Needs long walks and enjoys playing games.

Attitude to
OWNERS **loyal, affectionate**
CHILDREN **good, may chase in play**
OTHER PETS **good, may chase**
STRANGERS **wary unless well socialized, territorial**
UNFAMILIAR DOGS **good if well socialized**

Perfect owner
Experienced, considerate owner who has plenty of energy for long walks, training and chase games, and who will enjoy the close bond.

Potential problems
May display aggression to strangers and other dogs. This is particularly a problem with white-coated German Shepherds. May chase things it should not.

⚠️ Considerable brushing is needed to remove dead hair. An owner should be prepared for loose hair around the house.

Hungarian Kuvasz

bold • courageous • protective • devoted • gentle • patient

SIZE **66–75 cm (26–29½ in)** • WEIGHT **30–52 kg (66–115 lb)** • COAT **Thick, slight wavy, coarse, medium length topcoat, fine woolly undercoat** • COLOUR **Pure white. Skin highly pigmented with patches of slate grey** • LIFESPAN **11–13 years** • In the 'Working' Class in the USA

Well built and powerful, the Kuvasz has a strong, protective nature. They are loyal and devoted to their owners and need plenty of socialization to keep them tolerant of strangers and other dogs.

ORIGINALLY BRED to guard livestock.

Special characteristics
The Kuvasz has a strong guarding instinct.

Exercise requirements
Medium. Needs a fair amount of exercise.

Attitude to
OWNERS **loyal, affectionate**
CHILDREN **natural guards**
OTHER PETS **good if raised with them**
STRANGERS **suspicious, territorial**
UNFAMILIAR DOGS **can be problematic**

Perfect owner
Experienced, strong-willed, physically strong owner with a secure garden or yard who is willing to give this powerful dog a job to do to keep its lively mind occupied.

Potential problems
May display aggression towards strangers and unfamiliar dogs, and status-related aggression towards gentle owners.

⚠ Daily grooming is required to keep the thick coat in good condition. An owner should be prepared for loose hair in the house.

Pastoral

Hungarian Puli

lively • wary of strangers • responsive

SIZE **37–44 cm (14½–17½ in)** • WEIGHT **10–15 kg (22–33 lb)** • COAT **Corded coat, which may grow down to the ground** • COLOUR **Black, rusty black, white and various shades of grey and apricot** • LIFESPAN **12–13 years**

Pastoral

Lively and responsive, the Hungarian Puli is a natural guard. Although its distinctive corded coat may protect it from extremes of weather in its native land, a pet dog may be more comfortable and less smelly if clipped.

ORIGINALLY BRED to herd sheep.

Special characteristics
This dog has a protective nature, and likes to chase.

Exercise requirements
High. Enjoys playing.

Attitude to
OWNERS **loyal, affectionate**
CHILDREN **natural guard**
OTHER PETS **may chase**
STRANGERS **suspicious, territorial**
UNFAMILIAR DOGS **can be problematic**

Perfect owner
Experienced, sensible owner who has the time and energy for training and playing.

Potential problems
May bark excessively. Lack of activity may lead to problems, and some dogs may be aggressive to strangers.

⚠ The corded coat needs assistance to form dreadlocks as otherwise it will mat.

The corded coat helps to protect against extreme weather conditions when working.

Komondor

protective • wary of strangers • courageous • devoted

SIZE 60–80 cm (23½–31½ in) • WEIGHT 36–61 kg (80–135 lb) • COAT Corded coat, which may grow down to the ground • COLOUR White • LIFESPAN 12 years • In the 'Working' Class in the USA

Alert and protective, Komondors make loyal, independent guard dogs. Although its distinctive corded coat may protect it from extremes of weather in its native land, a pet dog may be more comfortable and less smelly if clipped.

ORIGINALLY BRED for guarding flocks of sheep from wolves.

Special characteristics
The Komondor is a protective dog.

Exercise requirements
Medium.

Attitude to
OWNERS loyal, affectionate
CHILDREN natural guard
OTHER PETS good if raised with them
STRANGERS wary, territorial
UNFAMILIAR DOGS can be problematic

Perfect owner
Experienced, sensible owner who has time and energy for training and coat care.

Potential problems
Tends to be aggressive to strangers and other dogs.

⚠️ Corded coat needs assistance to form dreadlocks as otherwise it will mat.

Pastoral

Lancashire Heeler

courageous • happy • alert • playful • affectionate

SIZE **26–30 cm (10–12 in)** • WEIGHT **3–6 kg (6–12 lb)** • COAT **Short, thick, hard topcoat with fine undercoat** • COLOUR **Black or liver with rich tan markings** • LIFESPAN **12–13 years**

Pastoral

Lancashire Heelers have strong herding instincts and may try to round up errant children or dogs with a well-aimed nip at the heels. Alert and playful, they are constantly busy with abundant energy.

ORIGINALLY BRED to herd cattle and catch rats and rabbits.

Special characteristics
This playful dog likes to chase and nip.

Exercise requirements
High. Tends to be busy indoors as well as out.

Attitude to
OWNERS loyal, affectionate
CHILDREN good if raised with them, may nip in play
OTHER PETS may be problematic with small pets
STRANGERS wary but friendly if well socialized
UNFAMILIAR DOGS good if well socialized

Perfect owner
Active, sensible owner who can provide an outlet for this dog's boundless energy and desire to play and be busy.

Potential problems
Nipping heels in play. May display aggression to strangers if not well socialized.

Maremma Sheepdog

strong-willed • aloof • independent • courageous

SIZE 60–73 cm (23½–28½ in) • WEIGHT 30–45 kg (66–99 lb) • COAT Long, plentiful and rather harsh with thick, close undercoat • COLOUR All white • LIFESPAN 10–12 years

Strong, powerful Maremmas are naturally protective and need plenty of socialization to ensure they are tolerant of strangers and other dogs. They have an independent, aloof nature and a thick coat that will shed hair in a warm house.

ORIGINALLY BRED to guard sheep from wolves.

Special characteristics
The Maremma has a very protective nature.

Exercise requirements
Medium. Not very energetic, but muscular so needs good walks.

Attitude to
OWNERS loyal, affectionate
CHILDREN natural guard
OTHER PETS good if raised with them
STRANGERS wary, territorial
UNFAMILIAR DOGS can be problematic

Perfect owner
Experienced, strong-willed, physically strong owner with a secure garden or yard who can give this powerful dog a job to do to keep its lively mind occupied.

Potential problems
Tends to be aggressive to strangers and unfamiliar dogs, and may display status-related aggression towards gentle owners.

⚠ Daily grooming is required to hair in good condition.

Pastoral

Norwegian Buhund

alert • courageous • energetic • independent • playful • curious

SIZE 41–45 cm (16–18 in) • WEIGHT 24–26 kg (53–58 lb) • COAT Outer coat smooth, harsh, with soft, woolly undercoat • COLOUR Wheaten, black, red, (red not too dark), wolf-sable • LIFESPAN 12–15 years

Pastoral

Once a farm dog, the Buhund has a strong chasing instinct and abundant energy. Curious and playful, they enjoy barking and need to live an active, busy life to prevent boredom.

ORIGINALLY BRED to herd sheep and cattle and to guard farms.

Special characteristics
This active and playful dog has a protective nature, and likes to chase.

Exercise requirements
High. Thoroughly enjoys being exercised.

Attitude to
OWNERS loyal, responsive
CHILDREN good
OTHER PETS good, may chase
STRANGERS will bark but friendly
UNFAMILIAR DOGS good

Perfect owner
Active, sensible owner who enjoys exercising, playing and training.

Potential problems
May bark excessively, and chase things it should not.

Old English Sheepdog

biddable • bold • faithful • affectionate

SIZE 56–61 cm (22–24 in) • WEIGHT 29.5–30.5 kg (65–67 lb) • COAT Profuse, of good harsh texture, with thick undercoat • COLOUR Any shade of grey, grizzle or blue. Body and hindquarters of solid colour with or without white socks • LIFESPAN 12–13 years

Lively, playful Old English Sheepdogs have a massive coat. Prolonged daily grooming is needed if they are to remain tangle-free and pet dogs may be more comfortable and more manageable if they are clipped, especially in summer.

ORIGINALLY BRED to herd sheep.

Special characteristics
The Old English Sheepdog likes to chase.

Exercise requirements
Medium. Joins in with enthusiasm.

Attitude to
OWNERS loyal, affectionate
CHILDREN good, may be clumsy with young children
OTHER PETS good, may chase
STRANGERS usually friendly
UNFAMILIAR DOGS good if well socialized

Perfect owner
Active, confident owner who has plenty of time for exercise, play, training and coat care.

Potential problems
Dogs from some lines may display possessive aggression over toys or food.

Pastoral

⚠ This dog's coat requires prolonged daily grooming to keep it in good condition. The hair above its eyes needs to be tied back so that the dog can see clearly.

Polish Lowland Sheepdog

lively • watchful • bright • clever • perceptive • alert • composed

SIZE 42–50 cm (16½–20 in) • WEIGHT 14–16 kg (30–35 lb) • COAT Long, dense, shaggy, thick coat of harsh texture with soft undercoat • COLOUR All colours acceptable • LIFESPAN 13–14 years

Pastoral

Lively and agile, Polish Lowland Sheepdogs need a job to do to keep them happy. They are responsive and affectionate with owners, but can be wary of strangers so early socialization is important.

ORIGINALLY BRED for herding livestock.

Special characteristics

This dog is curious by nature, and likes to chase.

Exercise requirements

Medium – High. Enjoys play and exercise.

Attitude to

OWNERS affectionate, responsive
CHILDREN good if socialized with them
OTHER PETS good, may chase
STRANGERS suspicious, territorial
UNFAMILIAR DOGS good well socialized

Perfect owner

Active, strong-willed owner who has plenty of energy to exercise, train and play with this active dog.

Potential problems

Tends to be aggressive to strangers. May be problematic if under-exercised.

⚠️ The long hair above its eyes needs to be cut or tied back so the dog can see clearly.

Pyrenean Mountain Dog

alert • confident • patient • steady • courageous

SIZE 65–81 cm (26–32 in) • WEIGHT 45–60 kg (90–132 lb) • COAT Profuse undercoat of very fine hairs; outer coat longer, coarser-textured. Long, very dense woollier hair on rear of thighs giving pantaloon effect • COLOUR White or white with patches of badger, wolf-grey or pale yellow. Black nose and eye rims • LIFESPAN 9–11 years • ALSO KNOWN AS Great Pyrenees • In the 'Working' Class in the USA

Being bred for generations as a pet dog has toned down the natural guarding instincts of the Pyrenean Mountain Dogs, but they still have a tendency to protect their own, making continual socialization with strangers and other dogs essential. Powerful, loyal, and independent, they require daily coat care to keep them looking their best.

ORIGINALLY BRED to guard flocks of sheep.

Special characteristics
This dog is naturally protective.

Exercise requirements
Low. Tends to be calm in the house.

Attitude to
OWNERS loyal, independent
CHILDREN natural guard
OTHER PETS good if raised with them
STRANGERS suspicious, territorial
UNFAMILIAR DOGS can be problematic

Perfect owner
Experienced, strong-willed, active owner who has enough space for this large independent dog and the energy to look after its coat and keep it occupied and exercised.

Potential problems
Some lines show aggression to strangers and other dogs.

⚠ Daily coat care is needed, and this breed tends to shed loose hair in the house.

Pastoral

Pyrenean Sheepdog

alert • lively • wary of strangers

SIZE **38–48 cm (15–19 in)** • WEIGHT **8–15 kg (18–33 lb)** • COAT **Long or semi-long** • COLOUR **Various shades of fawn, light to dark grey, blue merle, slate blue or brindle, black or black and white** • LIFESPAN **12–13 years**

Pastoral

Active, lively and responsive, the Pyrenean Sheepdog has strong chase instincts and likes to work. Sensitive and wary, they require early socialization to ensure they are agreeable with strangers and other dogs.

ORIGINALLY BRED to guard and herd sheep.

Special characteristics
This sheepdog is a fast runner, and likes to chase.

Exercise requirements
High. Needs plenty of exercise and games.

Attitude to
OWNERS **affectionate, responsive**
CHILDREN **good if raised with them**
OTHER PETS **may chase**
STRANGERS **wary, territorial**
UNFAMILIAR DOGS **okay if well socialized**

Perfect owner
Active, experienced owner who will socialize this dog well and provide it with plenty of games and activity.

Potential problems
May be aggressive to strangers. May display chase problems.

Samoyed

alert • affectionate • good-natured • independent

SIZE **46–56 cm (18–22 in)** • WEIGHT **23–30 kg (50–66 lb)** • COAT **Thick, close, soft and short undercoat,** with harsh hair growing through • COLOUR **Pure white, white and biscuit, cream, outer coat silver-tipped** • LIFESPAN **12 years** • In the 'Working' Class in the USA

Bred to live in cold climates and herd reindeers, Samoyeds have thick coats that need a great deal of brushing and that can cause them to overheat in summer. Good-natured and affectionate, they are also independent and not necessarily responsive to requests.

ORIGINALLY BRED to herd and guard reindeer herds.

⚠ Daily prolonged grooming is needed to keep the heavy coat in good shape. The thick coat makes this dog prone to overheating in summer. Loose hair will be shed in the house.

Special characteristics
This lively dog likes to chase.

Exercise requirements
Medium. Enjoys exercise but likes to have human company.

Attitude to
OWNERS **affectionate, independent**
CHILDREN **good**
OTHER PETS **good**
STRANGER **friendly**
UNFAMILIAR DOGS **friendly**

Perfect owner
Sociable, easy-going families who will enjoy this dog's independent, engaging character.

Pastoral

Shetland Sheepdog

alert • gentle • active • affectionate • responsive • reserved

SIZE **36–37 cm (14–14½ in)** • WEIGHT **6–7 kg (14–16 lb)** • COAT Long, harsh-textured, straight topcoat, with soft, short undercoat. Mane and frill very abundant, forelegs well feathered • COLOUR Sable, tricolour, blue merle, black and white, black and tan • LIFESPAN 13–14 years

Pastoral

Reserved and prone to shyness, Shetland Sheepdogs are gentle, affectionate and close-bonding to owners. They are also sensitive and timid. Their coats will need daily attention to keep them tangle-free.

ORIGINALLY BRED to herd sheep.

Special characteristics
This sheepdog is gentle, reserved and sensitive.

Exercise requirements
Medium. Will take exercise if offered.

Attitude to
OWNERS affectionate, responsive
CHILDREN can be timid with boisterous children
OTHER PETS good, may chase
STRANGERS reserved, timid
UNFAMILIAR DOGS reserved

Perfect owner
Active, gentle owner who will appreciate this dog's sensitivities and devotion, and enjoy the constant grooming needed to keep its coat in good shape.

Potential problems
May bark if lonely. May suffer from noise phobias.

⚠ The profuse coat needs regular grooming to keep it tangle-free.

Swedish Lapphund

patient • kind • friendly • devoted • lively • alert • independent

SIZE 40–51 cm (16–20 in) • WEIGHT 19.5–20.5 kg (43–45 lb) • COAT Thick, medium length, longer on brisket, thighs and tail, forming a ruff round neck, with dense and finely curled undercoat • COLOUR Bear-brown, black, brown • LIFESPAN 12–13 years

Bred to herd and guard reindeer, Swedish Lapphunds have thick coats that would have protected them from cold climates, but which can prove too hot in summer. Lively and independent, these dogs are active, curious and prone to barking.

ORIGINALLY BRED to herd and guard reindeer.

Special characteristics
This active dog has a curious, energetic nature.

Exercise requirements
High. Enjoys exercise.

Attitude to
OWNERS affectionate, responsive
CHILDREN good
OTHER PETS good
STRANGERS friendly, will bark
UNFAMILIAR DOGS friendly

Perfect owner
Active, playful owner who will enjoy the independent, rather stubborn nature of this energetic dog.

Potential problems
Barking, especially when left alone.

⚠ Daily grooming is needed to keep the thick coat in good condition.

Pastoral

Swedish Vallhund

watchful • alert • energetic • friendly • eager to please • courageous

SIZE **31–35 cm (12–13¾ in)** • WEIGHT **11.5–16 kg (25–35 lb)** • COAT **Medium length, harsh topcoat with abundant, soft, woolly undercoat** • COLOUR **Steel grey, greyish-brown, greyish-yellow, reddish-yellow, reddish-brown** • LIFESPAN **12–14 years**

Pastoral

Swedish Vallhunds are strong, playful and vigorous. Bred to herd cattle, they have a tendency to nip at heels when excited, and need active, playful owners to channel their energy into more acceptable games.

ORIGINALLY BRED to herd and guard cattle and for vermin control on farms.

Special characteristics
The Swedish Vallhund is playful and energetic.

Exercise requirements
High. Needs to have its abundant energy channelled.

Attitude to
OWNERS affectionate, independent
CHILDREN good, may nip heels in play
OTHER PETS can be problematic
STRANGERS good if well socialized
UNFAMILIAR DOGS can be problematic

Perfect owner
Active, experienced owner who has plenty of free time for training, play and exercise.

Potential problems
Likely to nip heels in play or to see off strangers.

Welsh Corgi (Cardigan)

alert • active • steady • confident

SIZE **27–30 cm (10½–12 in)** • WEIGHT **11–17 kg (25–38 lb)** • COAT **Medium length, straight, of hard texture, with good undercoat** • COLOUR **Any, with or without white markings** • LIFESPAN **12–14 years**

Cardigan Corgis have a full tail and are slightly more easy-going than Pembroke Corgis. They can be reserved with strangers, courageous and determined, and they are playful and independent with owners.

ORIGINALLY BRED to drive cattle.

Special characteristics
This is a courageous and determined dog.

Exercise requirements
Medium.

Attitude to
OWNERS **affectionate, independent**
CHILDREN **good, but may nip ankles in play**
OTHER PETS **good, may chase**
STRANGERS **reserved**
UNFAMILIAR DOGS **good if well socialized**

Perfect owner
Experienced, easy-going owner who can provide exercise, play and training to ensure that nipping ankles does not become this dog's job.

Potential problems
Likely to nip heels in play or to see off strangers.

Pastoral

Welsh Corgi (Pembroke)

bold • outgoing • alert • active • steady • confident

SIZE **25–30 cm (10–12 in)** • WEIGHT **9–12 kg (20–26 lb)** • COAT **Medium length, straight with dense undercoat** • COLOUR **Red, sable, fawn, black and tan** • LIFESPAN **12–14 years**

Pastoral

Pembrokes are born without a tail and have a character that is wilful, determined and reckless. Reserved with strangers, they make good watchdogs, but can be snappy when defending property unless they have been properly socialized.

ORIGINALLY BRED **to drive cattle.**

Special characteristics
This corgi is by nature courageous and determined.

Exercise requirements
Medium.

Attitude to
OWNERS **affectionate, independent**
CHILDREN **good, may nip ankles in play**
OTHER PETS **good, may chase**
STRANGERS **reserved**
UNFAMILIAR DOGS **good if well socialized**

Perfect owner
Experienced, strong-willed owner who can provide exercise, play and training to ensure that nipping ankles does not become this dog's job.

Potential problems
Likely to nip heels in play or to see off strangers.

Airedale Terrier

outgoing • confident • friendly • courageous • tenacious • stubborn

SIZE 56–61 cm (22–24 in) • WEIGHT 20–23 kg (44–50 lb) • COAT Hard, dense and wiry, with shorter, softer undercoat • COLOUR Tan with black saddle, top of the neck and top surface of tail also black • LIFESPAN 10–13 years

Airedales are feisty, easily aroused and courageous. With owners they are affectionate but independent, and early training and socialization is important to ensure these large terriers are well behaved with other dogs.

ORIGINALLY BRED to hunt and kill badgers and otters.

Special characteristics
The Airedale is feisty and easily aroused.

Exercise requirements
High. This is the largest of the terriers and needs plenty of exercise.

Attitude to
OWNERS affectionate, independent
CHILDREN good if raised with them
OTHER PETS may kill small pets, may injure cats unless raised with them
STRANGERS friendly if well socialized
UNFAMILIAR DOGS can be problematic

Perfect owner
Experienced, strong-willed, active owner who has plenty of time for playing and exercising this independent, powerful character.

 Regular grooming and clipping is needed to keep the coat in good order.

Potential problems
There may be control problems unless owners are able to win cooperation.

Terriers

American Staffordshire Terrier

loyal • obedient • feisty • tenacious • independent • affectionate

SIZE **43–48 cm (17–19 in)** • WEIGHT **18–23 kg (40–50 lb)** • COAT **Short, sleek** • COLOUR **Any**
• LIFESPAN **12 years**

Terriers

Taller and heavier than its English ancestor, American Staffordshire Terriers are feisty and tenacious. Easily aroused, they have tremendous jaw strength and continued socialization is needed to ensure they remain well behaved with other dogs.

ORIGINALLY BRED for bull-baiting and dog-fighting.

Special characteristics
This terrier has tremendous jaw strength and the ability to hold on when biting, and is easily aroused.

Exercise requirements
High. Very active, and enjoys exercise.

Attitude to
OWNERS affectionate, loving
CHILDREN good if raised with them, hard play bite when young
OTHER PETS may kill small pets, may injure cats unless raised with them
STRANGERS usually friendly
UNFAMILIAR DOGS tendency to be aggressive.
Adequate early socialization needed

Perfect owner
Experienced, strong-willed active owner who has time and knowledge to teach this dog to be nice to other dogs when it is a puppy, and who can provide a great deal of affection, exercise and play when older.

Potential problems
A tendency to be aggressive to other dogs.

This dog's ears were cropped to make them stand upright, but this is illegal in some countries.

Australian Terrier

alert • active • loyal • friendly • extrovert • obedient • courageous

SIZE **24.5–25.5 cm (10 in)** • WEIGHT **5–6.5 kg (14 lb)** • COAT **Harsh, straight, dense topcoat, with short, soft-textured undercoat** • COLOUR **Blue, sandy or red** • LIFESPAN **14 years**

Australian Terriers are high energy workers. Easily aroused by quick movement, these dogs are alert, courageous hunters, and need plenty to do and a great deal of exercise to keep them happy.

ORIGINALLY BRED to hunt and kill rats.

Special characteristics
This terrier is quick, alert and excited by quick movement, and easily aroused.

Exercise requirements
High. Needs plenty of exercise to burn off abundant energy.

Attitude to
OWNERS **affectionate, biddable**
CHILDREN **good if raised with them**
OTHER PETS **may kill small pets, may injure cats unless raised with them**
STRANGERS **good**
UNFAMILIAR DOGS **can be problematic**

Perfect owner
Experienced owner who can provide an outlet for this dog's high energy levels through games, play and exercise.

Potential problems
May be aggressive to other dogs unless well socialized.

Terriers

Bedlington Terrier

spirited • calm • confident • affectionate • dignified • courageous

SIZE **38–43 cm (15–17 in)** • WEIGHT **8–10 kg (18–23 lb)** • COAT **Thick and linty** • COLOUR **Blue, liver, or sandy with or without tan** • LIFESPAN **14–15 years**

Graceful and lamb-like, Bedlington Terriers are calm and sweet-natured with owners, and spirited and playful when given the chance. They are reserved with strangers and need plenty of socialization to help them feel at ease.

ORIGINALLY BRED to hunt and kill rats and badgers.

Special characteristics
This feisty and tenacious terrier is easily aroused.

Exercise requirements
High. Enjoys exercise outside, but calm at home.

Attitude to
OWNERS **affectionate, biddable**
CHILDREN **good if raised with them**
OTHER PETS **may kill small pets, may injure cats unless raised with them**
STRANGERS **reserved**
UNFAMILIAR DOGS **good if well socialized**

Perfect owner
Active, calm owner who can provide plenty of stimulation through exercise and play for this dog 'in sheep's clothing'.

⚠ Regular grooming and clipping are needed to keep the coat in good order.

Border Terrier

active • sensible • kind • affectionate • devoted

SIZE **25–28 cm (10–11 in)** • WEIGHT **5–7 kg (11½–15½ lb)** • COAT **Harsh and dense, with close undercoat**
• COLOUR **Red, wheaten, grizzle and tan, or blue and tan** • LIFESPAN **13–14 years**

Sweet-natured and affectionate, Border Terriers can be happy lying beside the fire or going out all day on long walks. Alert and playful, they are usually friendly and easy going with strangers and other dogs, and are also good watchdogs, without excessive barking.

ORIGINALLY BRED to hunt and kill rats and to dig foxes from lairs.

Special characteristics
This terrier is alert, easily aroused and playful.

Exercise requirements
Medium. Enjoys exercise but will not demand it.

Attitude to
OWNERS **affectionate, loyal**
CHILDREN **good**
OTHER PETS **can be problematic with small pets**
STRANGERS **good**
UNFAMILIAR DOGS **good if well socialized**

Perfect owner
Easy-going families without small pets who will enjoy exercising and playing with this sweet-natured little dog.

Terriers

✔ Recommended for first-time owners who do not keep small pets. The coat requires hand-stripping every 6 months.

Bull Terrier (English)

courageous • feisty • tenacious • obsessive • obstinate

SIZE **53–56 cm (21–22 in)** • WEIGHT **24–28 kg (52–62 lb)** • COAT **Short, flat, glossy** • COLOUR **White, black, brindle, red, fawn and tricolour** • LIFESPAN **11–13 years**

Terriers

Exuberant and powerful, English Bull Terriers are courageous and have strong jaws. With their high pain threshold and hard bite, they play roughly, and careful training and socialization is needed to prevent this becoming a problem. They are usually friendly with people, but early socialization is needed to ensure they remain tolerant of other dogs.

ORIGINALLY BRED for dog-fighting.

Special characteristics
Tenacious and courageous, English Bull Terriers have a strong bite.

Exercise requirements
Medium. Expect explosive bursts of energy.

Attitude to
OWNERS affectionate, devoted
CHILDREN good if raised with them
OTHER PETS may kill small pets, may injure cats unless raised with them
STRANGERS good if well socialized
UNFAMILIAR DOGS can be problematic. Adequate early socialization is required

Perfect owner
Experienced, active owner who has time and energy to play, train and exercise this powerful lovable character safely.

Potential problems
Tendency to be aggressive to other dogs unless well socialized. Dogs from some lines may display tail-chasing and other repetitive movement disorders. Lack of exercise may lead to destructiveness.

⚠ White dogs will need protection in high ultraviolet conditions to avoid sunburn on exposed pink areas of skin.

Bull Terrier (Miniature)

courageous • feisty • tenacious • playful • obsessive • obstinate

SIZE 25–35 cm (10–14 in) • WEIGHT 11–15 kg (24–33 lb) • COAT Short, flat, glossy • COLOUR White, black, brindle, red, fawn and tricolour • LIFESPAN 11–13 years

Miniature versions of the English Bull Terrier, these dogs also have exuberance and the same determination. With their high pain threshold and hard bite, they play roughly and careful training and socialization is needed to prevent this becoming a problem. They are usually friendly with people, but early socialization is needed to ensure they remain tolerant of other dogs.

ORIGINALLY BRED for dog-fighting, hunting, and killing rats.

Special characteristics
This dog is tenacious and courageous, with a strong bite.

Exercise requirements
Medium. Expect explosive bursts of energy.

⚠️ White dogs will need protection in high ultraviolet conditions to avoid sunburn on exposed pink areas of skin.

Attitude to
OWNERS affectionate, devoted, independent
CHILDREN good if raised with them
OTHER PETS may kill small pets, may injure cats unless raised with them
STRANGERS good if well socialized
UNFAMILIAR DOGS can be problematic. Adequate early socialization is required

Perfect owner
Experienced, active owner who has time and energy to play, train and exercise these determined dogs.

Potential problems
Tendency to be aggressive to other dogs unless well socialized. Dogs from some lines may display tail-chasing and other repetitive movement disorders. Lack of exercise may lead to destructive problems.

Terriers

Cairn Terrier

courageous • tenacious • sensible • confident • feisty • stubborn

SIZE 28–31 cm (11–12 in) • WEIGHT 6–7.5 kg (14–16 lb) • COAT Abundant harsh outer coat with short, soft undercoat • COLOUR Cream, wheaten, red, grey or nearly black • LIFESPAN 14–15 years

Terriers

Intense and inquisitive, Cairn Terriers are confident, feisty and playful. They are usually friendly to all, but quick to defend themselves if they feel threatened. Busy and active in the house, they will always be curious about what their owners are doing.

ORIGINALLY BRED to hunt and kill foxes, otters and weasels in rock piles (cairns) on Scottish farms.

Special characteristics
This terrier is alert and curious, and has a hard bite.

Exercise requirements
Medium. Busy at home and outside.

Attitude to
OWNERS affectionate, devoted
CHILDREN good if raised with them
OTHER PETS may kill small pets, may injure cats unless raised with them
STRANGERS good
UNFAMILIAR DOGS good if socialized

Perfect owner
Patient, fun-loving owner with tolerant neighbours who has time to play and exercise this active dog.

Potential problems
Tendency to bark excessively. Lack of exercise may lead to digging. May display possessiveness over toys and food.

Cesky Terrier

hardy • tough • feisty • persistent • stubborn • inquisitive

SIZE **28–35.5 cm (11–14 in)** • WEIGHT **7–8 kg (15½–17½ lb)** • COAT **Wavy with silky sheen** • COLOUR **Grey-blue or light brown** • LIFESPAN **12–14 years**

Curious, inquisitive Cesky Terriers are devoted to their owners, but reserved with strangers and make good watchdogs. Feisty and courageous, they need plenty of early socialization to ensure they are tolerant of strangers and other dogs.

ORIGINALLY BRED to dig out and kill rats and foxes.

Special characteristics
This terrier has a hard bite, and is easily aroused.

Exercise requirements
Medium. Enjoys exercising with owner.

Attitude to
OWNERS **affectionate, devoted**
CHILDREN **good if raised with them**
OTHER PETS **may kill small pets, may injure cats unless raised with them**
STRANGERS **reserved**
UNFAMILIAR DOGS **good if well socialized**

Perfect owner
Active, gentle owner who has time to socialize this dog well as a puppy and provide plenty of play and exercise when older.

Potential problems
May be snappy with strangers if undersocialized. Lack of exercise may lead to digging and destructiveness.

Terriers

⚠️ Regular grooming and clipping are needed to keep the coat in good order.

Dandie Dinmont Terrier

tenacious • stubborn • independent • sensitive • affectionate • calm • easy-going

SIZE **20–28 cm (8–11 in)** • WEIGHT **8–11 kg (18–24 lb)** • COAT **Hard topcoat with soft linty undercoat**
• COLOUR **Pepper or mustard** • LIFESPAN **15–16 years**

Terriers

Independent and sometimes a bit stubborn, Dandie Dinmont Terriers are loyal and affectionate to their owners, but reserved with strangers. Courageous and easily aroused, they require plenty of socialization when young.

ORIGINALLY BRED to dig out and kill foxes, weasels, badgers and rats.

Special characteristics
This dog is courageous and easily aroused, and has a hard bite.

Exercise requirements
Low. Enjoys playing.

Attitude to
OWNERS affectionate, loyal
CHILDREN good if raised with them
OTHER PETS may kill small pets, may injure cats unless raised with them
STRANGERS reserved
UNFAMILIAR DOGS friendly if well socialized

Perfect owner
Experienced, strong-willed affectionate owner who can provide plenty of play and attention to focus this wilful, protective dog.

Potential problems
May be aggressive to strangers if not well socialized. Some dogs may display status-related aggression to gentle owners.

Fox Terrier

Fox terriers are quick, alert, curious and active. They are good watchdogs and need plenty to do to stop them from getting into mischief. Affectionate, but independent with owners, these extrovert dogs are usually friendly with strangers, but careful socialization is needed to ensure they are tolerant of other dogs. Care is needed with small pets as their desire to hunt and kill small prey is strong.

Smooth

alert • quick • keen • friendly • extrovert • obstinate • curious

SIZE 38.5–39.5 cm (14–15 in) • WEIGHT 7–8 kg (15–18 lb) • COAT Straight, smooth, hard • COLOUR White should predominate, all white, white with tan, black and tan or black markings • LIFESPAN 13–14 years

ORIGINALLY BRED to hunt foxes, and hunt and kill rabbits and rats.

Special characteristics
The Fox Terrier is alert and easily aroused, with a hard bite.

Exercise requirements
High. Busy at home, active on walks.

Attitude to
OWNERS affectionate, independent
CHILDREN good if raised with them
OTHER PETS may kill small pets, may injure cats unless raised with them
STRANGERS friendly if well socialized, territorial
UNFAMILIAR DOGS can be problematic unless well socialized

Perfect owner
Active, experienced, strong-willed, playful owner who will enjoy the energy of this active, curious dog.

Potential problems
Tends to bark excessively and may be aggressive to other animals. May escape or dig if under-exercised.

Terriers

Wire-haired

alert • quick • keen • friendly • extrovert • obstinate • curious

SIZE **38.5–39.5 cm (14–15 in)** • WEIGHT **7–8 kg (15–18 lb)** • COAT **Dense, very wiry texture** • COLOUR **White should predominate, all white, white with tan, black and tan or black markings** • LIFESPAN **13–14 years**

Terriers

The Wire Fox Terrier is the rough-haired version of the Smooth Fox Terrier, and has a similar personality and characteristics.

ORIGINALLY BRED to hunt foxes, and hunt and kill rabbits and rats.

Special characteristics
Alert and easily aroused, this terrier has a hard bite.

Exercise requirements
High. Busy at home, active on walks.

Attitude to
OWNERS affectionate, independent
CHILDREN good if raised with them
OTHER PETS may kill small pets, may injure cats unless raised with them
STRANGERS friendly if well socialized, territorial
UNFAMILIAR DOGS can be problematic unless well socialized

Perfect owner
Active, experienced, strong-willed, playful owner who will enjoy the energy of this active, curious dog.

Potential problems
Tends to bark excessively and may be aggressive to other animals. May escape or dig if under-exercised.

Glen of Imaal Terrier

active • spirited • courageous • quiet • independent

SIZE 35–36 cm (14 in) • WEIGHT 15.5–16.5 kg (34–36 lb) • COAT Medium length, harsh texture with soft undercoat
• COLOUR Blue, brindle and wheaten (all shades) • LIFESPAN 13–14 years • In the 'Miscellaneous' class in the USA

Courageous and tenacious, Glen of Imaal Terriers are unlikely to back down if challenged. Affectionate, loyal and independent with owners, they are easily aroused and need plenty of socialization to keep them tolerant of other dogs.

ORIGINALLY BRED to hunt and kill foxes and badgers.

Special characteristics
Alert and easily aroused, this terrier has a hard bite.

Exercise requirements
High. Enjoys exercise.

Attitude to
OWNERS affectionate, loyal
CHILDREN good if raised with them
OTHER PETS may kill small pets, may injure cats unless raised with them
STRANGERS good if socialized well
UNFAMILIAR DOGS can be problematic

Perfect owner
Experienced, active owner who can provide plenty of safe exercise and play for this active, feisty, independent little dog.

Potential problems
Tendency to be aggressive towards other dogs.

Terriers

Irish Terrier

reckless • affectionate • courageous • devoted • good-tempered

SIZE **46–48 cm (18–19 in)** • WEIGHT **11–12 kg (25–27 lb)** • COAT **Harsh and wiry** • COLOUR **Red, red/wheaten, or yellow/red** • LIFESPAN **13 years**

Terriers

Similar in appearance to Airedales but smaller, Irish Terriers are good-natured with their owners and, usually, strangers. Feisty and easily aroused, they are reactive and problematic around other dogs and need plenty of early socialization to remain tolerant.

ORIGINALLY BRED to hunt and kill rats and rabbits.

Special characteristics

The Irish Terrier is fast and curious, with a hard bite.

Exercise requirements

High. Needs plenty of exercise in a safe environment.

Attitude to

OWNERS **affectionate, loyal**
CHILDREN **good if raised with them**
OTHER PETS **may kill small pets, may injure cats unless raised with them**
STRANGERS **territorial**
UNFAMILIAR DOGS **very problematic and aggressive. Needs adequate, early and continued socialization**

Perfect owner

Experienced, strong-willed active owner who has the time and knowledge to adequately socialize these dogs as puppies and provide games and safe exercise when they are older.

Potential problems

Tends to be aggressive to other dogs and strangers.

Jack Russell Terrier

active • resilient • courageous • tenacious • independent • feisty • exuberant

SIZE **23–26 cm (9–12 in)** • WEIGHT **4–7 kg (9–15 lb)** • COAT **Smooth-haired and rough-haired varieties known** • COLOUR **Any** • LIFESPAN **12–18 years**

Jack Russell Terriers are popular and well known. They are active, inquisitive and extrovert, as well as being easily aroused and unlikely to back down if challenged. They need careful socialization with children, adults and other dogs when young.

ORIGINALLY BRED to hunt and kill rats and mice.

Special characteristics
Jack Russells are alert and easily aroused, with a hard bite.

Exercise requirements
High. Needs plenty of exercise.

Attitude to
OWNERS affectionate, loyal
CHILDREN good if raised with them
OTHER PETS may kill small pets, may injure cats unless raised with them
STRANGERS good if well socialized
UNFAMILIAR DOGS can be problematic unless well socialized

Perfect owner
Experienced, active owner who has the knowledge and time to socialize this dog well when a puppy and provide plenty of activity, exercise and play when an adult.

Potential problems
May be aggressive to strangers and other dogs, tendency to be 'snappy'.

Terriers

Kerry Blue Terrier

alert • determined • tenacious • courageous • playful • active

SIZE **46–48 cm (18–19 in)** • WEIGHT **15–17 kg (33–37 lb)** • COAT **Non-shedding soft wavy topcoat with no undercoat** • COLOUR **Any shade of blue with or without black points** • LIFESPAN **14 years**

Terriers

Active, alert and curious, Kerry Blue Terriers are devoted and playful with their owners and people they know. Reserved with strangers, they make good watchdogs and need early and continued socialization, especially with other dogs.

ORIGINALLY BRED to hunt and kill rats and rabbits.

Attitude to

OWNERS **affectionate, devoted**
CHILDREN **good, protective**
OTHER PETS **may kill small pets, may injure cats unless raised with them**
STRANGERS **reserved, territorial**
UNFAMILIAR DOGS **likely to be problematic. Early and continued socialization needed**

Perfect owner

Experienced, active owner who can provide a safe outlet for this dog's high energy levels.

Potential problems

Tendency to be aggressive to other dogs, and may display status-related aggression towards gentle owners.

⚠ Coat will need regular grooming and clipping.

Special characteristics

These terriers are alert and easily aroused, and have a hard bite.

Exercise requirements

High. Playful and full of energy.

Lakeland Terrier

keen • quick • friendly • confident • courageous • tenacious • independent

SSIZE **33–37 cm (13–14½ in)** • WEIGHT **7–8 kg (15–17 lb)** • COAT **Dense, harsh and weather-resistant with good undercoat** • COLOUR **Black and tan, blue and tan, red, wheaten, red grizzle, liver, blue or black** • LIFESPAN **13–14 years**

Lakeland Terriers are alert, active and keen. They like to be busy and will find their own things to do if bored. More easy-going with other dogs than many other terriers, Lakelands are friendly with strangers and other dogs if they have been properly socialized.

ORIGINALLY BRED to hunt and kill rats, mice and rabbits.

Attitude to
OWNERS affectionate, loyal
CHILDREN good if raised with them
OTHER PETS may kill small pets, may injure cats unless raised with them
STRANGERS friendly if well socialized
UNFAMILIAR DOGS good if well socialized

Perfect owner
Active, playful owner who likes to include their dog in plenty of exercise and activity.

Potential problems
Tends to be aggressive to other dogs unless well socialized.

Special characteristics
This terrier is alert and easily aroused, with a hard bite.

Exercise requirements
High. Busy and loves plenty of exercise.

Terriers

Manchester Terrier

keen • alert • discerning • determined • tenacious • devoted

SIZE **38–41 cm (15–16 in)** • WEIGHT **5–10 kg (11–22 lb)** • COAT **Close, smooth, and glossy** • COLOUR **Jet black and rich mahogany tan** • LIFESPAN **13–14 years**

Terriers

Clean and cat-like, Manchester Terriers appear very delicate, but are robust and determined underneath. Active and curious, they have not lost their desire to hunt. They are wary and aloof with strangers, but affectionate and devoted to their owners.

ORIGINALLY BRED to hunt and kill rats and rabbits.

Special characteristics
The Manchester Terrier is alert and easily aroused, and has a hard bite.

Exercise requirements
Medium. Active and likes to be entertained.

Attitude to
OWNERS affectionate, devoted
CHILDREN good if raised with them
OTHER PETS may kill small pets, may injure cats unless raised with them
STRANGERS wary, aloof
UNFAMILIAR DOGS good if well socialized

Perfect owner
Gentle, playful experienced owner who can provide enough activity to keep this active dog entertained and who will enjoy its independent nature.

Potential problems
Tends to bark excessively. Lack of exercise may lead to escapes.

Manchester Terriers, unlike the smaller English Toy Terrier, have ears that fold over and hang down.

Norfolk Terrier

alert • good-natured • tenacious • courageous • independent • lively

SIZE **24–25 cm (9–10 in)** • WEIGHT **5–5.5 kg (11–12 lb)** • COAT **Hard, wiry, medium length, straight** • COLOUR **All shades of red, wheaten, black and tan or grizzle** • LIFESPAN **14 years**

Norfolk Terriers are similar to Norwich Terriers, but have folded ears, giving them a softer appearance. They are feisty little hunters, good watchdogs, responsive and loyal to their owners and usually friendly with strangers and other dogs, although proper socialization is essential.

ORIGINALLY BRED to hunt and kill rats.

Special characteristics
This terrier is alert and easily aroused, with a hard bite.

Exercise requirements
Medium. Enjoys rough-and-tumble play.

Attitude to
OWNERS affectionate, loyal
CHILDREN good if raised with them
OTHER PETS may kill small pets, may chase cats unless raised with them
STRANGERS friendly
UNFAMILIAR DOGS friendly if well socialized

Perfect owner
Active, easy-going owner who will provide plenty of play and exercise for this exuberant, independent little dog.

⚠ Coat needs hand-stripping or clipping twice a year.

Terriers

Norwich Terrier

alert • good-natured • tenacious • courageous • independent • lively

SIZE **24–25 cm (9–10 in)** • WEIGHT **5–5.5 kg (11–12 lb)** • COAT **Hard, wiry, medium length, straight** • COLOUR **All shades of red, wheaten, black and tan or grizzle** • LIFESPAN **14 years**

Terriers

Norwich Terriers are similar to Norfolk Terriers, but have pricked ears. They are feisty little hunters, good watchdogs, responsive and loyal to their owners and usually friendly with strangers and other dogs, although proper socialization is essential.

ORIGINALLY BRED to hunt and kill rats.

Special characteristics
The Norwich Terrier is alert and easily aroused, and has a hard bite.

Exercise requirements
Medium. Enjoys play.

Attitude to
OWNERS **affectionate, loyal**
CHILDREN **good if raised with them**
OTHER PETS **may kill small pets, may chase cats unless raised with them**
STRANGERS **friendly**
UNFAMILIAR DOGS **friendly if well socialized**

Perfect owner
Active, easy-going owner who will provide plenty of play and exercise for this exuberant, independent little dog.

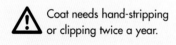
⚠ Coat needs hand-stripping or clipping twice a year.

Parson Russell Terrier

bold • friendly • tenacious • courageous • spirited

SIZE **33–36 cm (13–14 in)** • WEIGHT **5–8 kg (12–19 lb)** • COAT **Naturally harsh, dense, whether rough or smooth** • COLOUR **Entirely white or predominantly white with tan, lemon or black markings** • LIFESPAN **13–14 years**

The show cousin of the Jack Russell Terrier, Parson Russell Terriers are lively, active and curious. They are easily aroused extroverts, unlikely to back down if challenged and need careful socialization with children, adults and other dogs when young.

ORIGINALLY BRED to follow the hunt and dig out foxes from their lairs.

Special characteristics
This dog is feisty and easily aroused, with a hard bite.

Exercise requirements
High. Needs plenty of exercise to burn off its abundant energy.

Attitude to
OWNERS affectionate, loyal
CHILDREN good if raised with them
OTHER PETS may kill small pets, may injure cats unless raised with them
STRANGERS good if well socialized
UNFAMILIAR DOGS good if well socialized

Perfect owner
Active, tolerant, playful owner who can provide energetic walks and enough playful activity to use up this lively dog's mental and physical energy.

Potential problems
Tends to bark excessively. May be 'snappy' if inadequately socialized, especially with other dogs.

Terriers

Scottish Terrier

dignified • sensible • independent • reserved • courageous • bold • stubborn

SIZE 25–28 cm (10–11 in) • WEIGHT 8.5–10.5 kg (19–23 lb) • COAT Harsh, dense and wiry topcoat, with short, dense and soft undercoat • COLOUR Black, wheaten or brindle of any shade • LIFESPAN 13–14 years

Terriers

Wilful and independent, the Scottish Terrier is courageous and unlikely to back down if challenged. Loyal to their owners, Scotties need plenty of early socialization with people and other dogs.

ORIGINALLY BRED to hunt and kill small mammals.

Special characteristics
Feisty and easily aroused, the Scottish Terrier has a hard bite.

Exercise requirements
Medium. Needs exercise to burn off energy.

Attitude to
OWNERS **affectionate, loyal**
CHILDREN **tolerant if raised with them**
OTHER PETS **may kill small pets, may injure cats unless raised with them**
STRANGERS **reserved, territorial**
UNFAMILIAR DOGS **can be problematic**

Perfect owner
Experienced, strong-willed, determined owner who can match this dog's personality and who is willing to provide plenty of safe activity to use up its energy.

Potential problems
May display status-related aggression with gentle owners. Tends to be aggressive to strangers and other dogs if inadequately socialized.

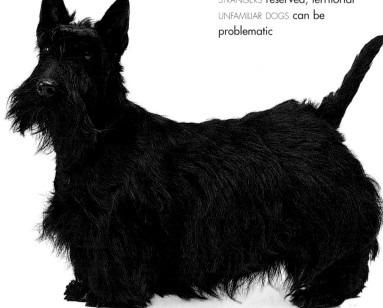

⚠ Coat needs hand-stripping or clipping twice a year.

Sealyham Terrier

alert • courageous • friendly • tenacious • stubborn • independent

SIZE **25–31 cm (10–12 in)** • WEIGHT **8–9 kg (18–20 lb)** • COAT **Long, hard and wiry topcoat with thick undercoat** • COLOUR **All white or white with lemon, brown, blue or badger pied markings on head and ears** • LIFESPAN **14 years**

Wilful and independent, Sealyhams have plenty of self-assurance. They are loyal and affectionate watchdogs, have retained a strong hunting instinct and need plenty of activity to keep them occupied.

ORIGINALLY BRED **to hunt and kill badgers and otters.**

Special characteristics
The Sealyham is feisty and easily aroused, with a hard bite.

Exercise requirements
Medium. Needs exercise to burn off energy.

Attitude to
OWNERS **affectionate, loyal**
CHILDREN **good if raised with them**
OTHER PETS **may kill small pets, may injure cats unless raised with them**
STRANGERS **reserved, territorial**
UNFAMILIAR DOGS **can be problematic**

Perfect owner
Experienced, strong-willed, active owner able to enjoy this independent character and provide plenty of activity and play to use up its energy.

Potential problems
May display status-related aggression with gentle owners. Tends to be aggressive to strangers and other dogs if inadequately socialized.

Terriers

Skye Terrier

dignified • mistrustful of strangers • tenacious • bold • confident • independent

SIZE 25–26 cm (9–10 in) • WEIGHT 8.5–10.5 kg (19–23 lb) • COAT Long, hard outer coat, with short, soft, woolly undercoat • COLOUR Black, dark or light grey, fawn, cream, all with black points • LIFESPAN 13 years

Terriers

Skye Terriers have a coat that needs care and attention to keep it free of tangles. They are reserved and territorial with strangers, but affectionate and loyal to owners. They have retained a strong desire to hunt, and need careful socialization to ensure they are tolerant with strangers and other dogs.

ORIGINALLY BRED to hunt and kill otter, badger and weasel.

Special characteristics
This terrier is alert and easily aroused, with a hard bite.

Exercise requirements
Medium.

Attitude to
OWNERS affectionate, loyal
CHILDREN good if raised with them
OTHER PETS may kill small pets, may injure cats unless raised with them
STRANGERS reserved, territorial
UNFAMILIAR DOGS can be problematic

Perfect owner
Experienced, strong-willed, active owner able to enjoy this independent character and provide plenty of socialization when young and activity when older.

Potential problems
Tendency to be aggressive to strangers. May display status-related aggression to gentle owners.

⚠ Daily coat care is needed to prevent tangling. Hair should be cut or tied up out of the eyes so this dog can see clearly.

Soft Coated Wheaten Terrier

good-tempered • spirited • confident • affectionate • independent

SIZE 46–49 cm (18–19½ in) • WEIGHT 16–20.5 kg (35–45 lb) • COAT Soft and silky • COLOUR A good clear wheaten • LIFESPAN 13–14 years

High-spirited Soft Coated Wheaten Terriers are good-tempered, but can be wilful and independent. They are active and playful with owners and have a coat that will need careful cleaning after a long, boisterous walk.

ORIGINALLY BRED for droving, herding and hunting.

Attitude to

OWNERS affectionate, loyal
CHILDREN good if raised with them
OTHER PETS may kill small pets, may injure cats unless raised with them
STRANGERS good if well socialized
UNFAMILIAR DOGS can be problematic

Perfect owner

Experienced, strong-willed owner who can provide this exuberant dog with a job to do, plenty of exercise, play and training.

Potential problems

May display status-related aggression to gentle owners, and tends to be aggressive to other dogs.

Special characteristics

This terrier is active, playful and versatile.

Exercise requirements

High. Enjoys plenty of exercise.

⚠ The dog's coat will bring in mud and dirt from outside and will need careful cleaning.

Staffordshire Bull Terrier

courageous • tenacious • affectionate • bold • feisty

SIZE **36–41 cm (14–16 in)** • WEIGHT **11–17 kg (24–38 lb)** • COAT **Smooth, short and close** • COLOUR **Red, fawn, white, black or blue, or any one of these colours with white. Any shade of brindle or any shade of brindle with white** • LIFESPAN **11–12 years**

Terriers

Staffordshire Bull Terriers are feisty and tenacious. Easily aroused, they have tremendous jaw strength and early and continued socialization is needed to ensure they remain well behaved with others, especially with other dogs.

ORIGINALLY BRED for dog-fighting.

Special characteristics
The Staffordshire Bull Terrier has tremendous jaw strength and the ability to hold on when biting; it is also easily aroused.

Exercise requirements
High. Will walk a long way if required.

Attitude to
OWNERS affectionate, loving
CHILDREN very good if raised with them, hard play bite when young
OTHER PETS may kill small pets, may injure cats unless raised with them
STRANGERS usually friendly
UNFAMILIAR DOGS tendency to be aggressive. Adequate early socialization needed

Perfect owner
Experienced, strong-willed, active owner who has the time and knowledge to teach this dog to be nice to other dogs when it is a puppy, and who can provide plenty of affection, exercise and play when older.

Potential problems
Tends to be aggressive to other dogs.

Welsh Terrier

sociable • curious • playful • tenacious

SIZE **36–39 cm (14–15½ in)** • WEIGHT **9–9.5 kg (20–21 lb)** • COAT **Wiry, hard, very close and abundant**
• COLOUR **Black and tan for preference, or black grizzle and tan** • LIFESPAN **14 years**

Welsh Terriers are active, curious and busy, always looking for something to do. Courageous and independent, they have not lost their hunting spirit and are unlikely to back down if challenged.

ORIGINALLY BRED to hunt and kill rats and other small animals.

Special characteristics
Alert and easily aroused, the Welsh Terrier has a hard bite.

Exercise requirements
Medium. Enjoys exercise and games.

Attitude to
OWNERS **affectionate, loyal**
CHILDREN **good if raised with them**
OTHER PETS **may kill small pets, may injure cats unless raised with them**
STRANGERS **can be wary, territorial**
UNFAMILIAR DOGS **can be problematic**

Perfect owner
Experienced, confident owner who has the time and energy to play, train and exercise a dog with an exuberant, independent character.

Potential problems
Tends to be aggressive to other dogs.

Terriers

 This dog's coat needs regular stripping or clipping to keep it in good condition.

West Highland White Terrier

confident • alert • courageous • independent • friendly

SIZE **25–28 cm (10–11 in)** • WEIGHT **7–10 kg (15–22 lb)** • COAT **Harsh topcoat with short, soft undercoat** • COLOUR **White** • LIFESPAN **14 years**

Terriers

Active and high spirited, West Highland White Terriers are popular pets. Feisty and easily aroused, they can also be wilful and independent. Westies are excellent watchdogs, but the desire to bark should be calmed early to prevent them becoming too noisy.

ORIGINALLY BRED **to hunt and kill rats.**

Special characteristics
The Westie is alert and easily aroused, with a hard bite.

Exercise requirements
High. Enjoys exercise and play.

Attitude to
OWNERS **affectionate, loyal**
CHILDREN **good if raised with them**
OTHER PETS **may kill small pets, may injure cats unless raised with them**
STRANGERS **friendly if well socialized**
UNFAMILIAR DOGS **friendly if well socialized**

Perfect owner
Strong-willed, active owner who will enjoy this dog's excitable, independent spirit and who can provide plenty of play, exercise and training.

Potential problems
Dogs from some lines may display status-related aggression towards gentle owners (especially male dogs). Tends to bark excessively.

 Coat will need to be clipped regularly.

Affenpinscher

busy • pushy • affectionate • curious • alert • fast • confident

SIZE **24–28 cm (9½–11 in)** • WEIGHT **3–4 kg (6½–9 lb)** • COAT **Hard, wiry, medium length** • COLOUR **Black, black and tan, red, brindle and tan** • LIFESPAN **14 years**

Monkeyish in looks and behaviour, Affenpinschers are wilful, stubborn and independent. They are lively and inquisitive, and have strong hunting instincts. They are reserved with strangers and make good little watchdogs.

ORIGINALLY BRED to catch rats and mice, later to be ladies' companions.

Special characteristics
The Affenpinscher is alert, reactive and playful.

Exercise requirements
Medium. Busy in the house and outside.

Attitude to
OWNERS **affectionate, independent**
CHILDREN **puppies and adults may be injured by boisterous children**
OTHER PETS **may be problematic with small pets**
STRANGERS **reserved, good watchdog**
UNFAMILIAR DOGS **good if well socialized**

Perfect owner
Confident owner who will enjoy the independent, wilful nature of this lively little dog and who can provide plenty of exercise and play.

Potential problems
May be difficult to housetrain and display status-related problems with gentle owners. May bark excessively.

⚠ This dog's shortened nose can make breathing difficult, and it is likely to snore.

The Affenpinscher's shortened face and bushy eyebrows give them a monkeyish appearance.

Toys

Australian Silky Terrier

energetic • determined • courageous • keen • alert • friendly • responsive

SIZE 22–23 cm (8–9 in) • WEIGHT 4–5 kg (8–10 lb) • COAT Long, fine and glossy, silky texture • COLOUR Blue and tan, grey-blue and tan, the richer these colours the better • LIFESPAN 14–16 years • ALSO KNOWN AS Silky Terrier

Toys

Energetic, alert and lively, Australian Silky Terriers make excellent watchdogs and care is needed to prevent their barking becoming excessive. They are friendly, responsive and playful.

ORIGINALLY BRED to be a watchdog and to kill rats and mice.

Special characteristics
This dog is alert, reactive and playful.

Exercise requirements
Medium. Busy both at home and outside.

Attitude to
OWNERS affectionate, independent
CHILDREN good, puppies are very small and may be injured by young children
OTHER PETS may be problematic with small pets
STRANGERS friendly
UNFAMILIAR DOGS good if well socialized

Perfect owner
Active, confident owner who will enjoy this dog's independent spirit and will be able to provide exercise, play and activities to keep this busy dog occupied.

Potential problems
May bark excessively. Tends to snap if frustrated or excited.

⚠️ The silky coat needs careful daily brushing to prevent mats from forming. There is no undercoat so the dog may be cold in winter.

Unlike those of the Yorkshire Terrier, the ears of the Australian Silky Terrier are free from long hair.

Bichon Frise

happy • lively • vivacious • affectionate

SIZE **23–28 cm (9–11 in)** • WEIGHT **3–6 kg (7–12 lb)** • COAT **Fine, silky with soft corkscrew curls**
• COLOUR **White** • LIFESPAN **14 years** • In the 'Non-sporting' class in the USA

Although their coats need daily care, Bichon Frise are good-natured dogs which make excellent pets. Lively and vivacious, they are friendly with everyone and they make easy, delightful companions.

ORIGINALLY BRED to be a companion.

Special characteristics
This is a friendly dog that enjoys human company.

Exercise requirements
Low – Medium. Enjoys playing family games.

Attitude to
OWNERS **affectionate, devoted**
CHILDREN **good**
OTHER PETS **good**
STRANGERS **friendly**
UNFAMILIAR DOGS **friendly**

Perfect owner
Sociable, affectionate owner who will enjoy the daily coat care ritual.

Potential problems
May be hard to housetrain.

Toys

⚠ This dog's coat will bring in mud and dirt from outside, and needs daily care and occasional clipping to keep it in good condition.

✔ Recommended for first-time owners who like to groom their dog on a daily basis.

Bolognese

devoted • affectionate to owners • serious • docile • reserved with strangers

SIZE **25.5–30.5 cm (10–12 in)** • WEIGHT **3–4 kg (5–9 lb)** • COAT **Long, flocked without curl covering entire head and body** • COLOUR **White. Lips, eyelids, nose and nails black** • LIFESPAN **14 years**

Toys

Similar to the Bichon Frise but more serious, shy and reserved with strangers. Bologneses like to form strong bonds with their owners, with whom they are affectionate and devoted.

ORIGINALLY BRED to be a companion.

Special characteristics
This gentle dog enjoys company.

Exercise requirements
Low. Enjoys free exercise.

Attitude to
OWNERS **affectionate, devoted**
CHILDREN **good**
OTHER PETS **good**
STRANGERS **reserved, shy**
UNFAMILIAR DOGS **friendly if well socialized**

Perfect owner
Gentle, affectionate, quiet-living owner.

Potential problems
May suffer from separation problems. May be hard to housetrain.

Cavalier King Charles Spaniel

sporting • lively • gentle • affectionate • friendly

SIZE 31–33 cm (12–13 in) • WEIGHT 5–8 kg (12–18 lb) • COAT Long, silky, with plenty of feathering
• COLOUR Black and tan, ruby, Blenheim (chestnut markings on white ground), tricolour • LIFESPAN 9–11 years

Happy and playful, Cavalier King Charles Spaniels make ideal companions. They are plagued with inherited health problems so finding a healthy strain is important. Devoted and affectionate with owners, they are friendly with all and make excellent pets for families with children.

ORIGINALLY BRED to be a companion.

Attitude to

OWNERS affectionate, devoted
CHILDREN playful, good-natured
OTHER PETS good
STRANGERS friendly
UNFAMILIAR DOGS friendly

Perfect owner

Affectionate, gentle families who will enjoy this lively, playful dog.

⚠️ Will bring mud and dirt in from outside on its coat.

✔️ Recommended for first-time owners who like to groom their dog on a daily basis. It is important to find a healthy dog.

Toys

Special characteristics

This spaniel is affectionate, sweet-natured and playful.

Exercise requirements

Medium. Enjoys and needs regular exercise.

Chihuahua (Longhaired, Smooth Coated)

alert • spirited • bold • friendly • affectionate

SIZE 15–23 cm (6–8 in) • WEIGHT 1–3 kg (2–6 lb) • COAT Long-haired: Medium length, soft texture
• Smooth Coated: Smooth, soft texture • COLOUR Any • LIFESPAN 14–18 years

Toys

Chihuahuas are big dogs in a little body. Bold and spirited, they are lively, and playful and devoted to their owners. They are also friendly to others, although naturally wary of boisterous children or dogs much larger than themselves.

ORIGINALLY BRED to be a companion.

Special characteristics
The Chihuahua is playful and likes human company.

Exercise requirements
Low. Enthusiastic about exercise.

Attitude to
OWNERS affectionate, devoted
CHILDREN puppies and adults may be injured by boisterous children
OTHER PETS good
STRANGERS friendly
UNFAMILIAR DOGS friendly

Perfect owner
Gentle, affectionate owner who will play with and take special care of this tiny dog.

Longhaired variety

Chinese Crested

Chinese Cresteds are bred in two varieties, the Hairless and Powder Puff. Chinese Cresteds are lively, affectionate pets which are devoted to their owners.

Hairless

lively • affectionate • sensitive • fun-loving • stubborn

SIZE **23–33 cm (9–13 in)** • WEIGHT **2–5.5 kg (5–12 lb)** • COAT **Soft, supple skin with long silky hair on the head, feet and tail** • COLOUR **Any** • LIFESPAN **15 years**

ORIGINALLY BRED to be a companion.

Special characteristics
The Chinese Crested is friendly, and likes to be with people.

Exercise requirements
Low.

Attitude to
OWNERS affectionate, devoted
CHILDREN puppies and adults may be injured by boisterous children
OTHER PETS good
STRANGERS friendly
UNFAMILIAR DOGS friendly if well socialized

Perfect owner
Sociable, affectionate owner who will happily perform daily skin care.

Potential problems
May be difficult to housetrain and prone to territory marking, particularly if male.

⚠ A daily skincare routine is needed for the Hairless variety, which can be prone to skin complaints. They may have missing teeth and toenails. Some young Hairless dogs can go through a 'teenage' acne stage. They also suffer from cold temperatures and get sunburned easily.

Powder Puff

lively • affectionate • sensitive • fun-loving • stubborn

SIZE 23–33 cm (9–13 in) • WEIGHT 2–5.5 kg (5–12 lb) • COAT Completely covered with long silky hair
• COLOUR Any • LIFESPAN 15 years

Toys

Cresteds are lively, affectionate dogs and are devoted to their owners.

ORIGINALLY BRED to be a companion.

Special characteristics
The Chinese Crested is friendly, and likes to be with people.

Exercise requirements
Low.

Attitude to
OWNERS affectionate, devoted
CHILDREN puppies and adults may be injured by boisterous children
OTHER PETS good
STRANGERS friendly
UNFAMILIAR DOGS friendly if well socialized

Perfect owner
Sociable, affectionate owner who will perform daily coat care.

Potential problems
May be difficult to housetrain and prone to territory marking, particularly if male.

⚠️ The Powder Puff variety will need daily grooming to keep its silky fur free of tangles.

The Powder Puff's face is usually shaved for shows.

English Toy Terrier (Black and Tan)

keen • alert • discerning • determined • tenacious • devoted

SIZE 25–30 cm (10–12 in) • WEIGHT 2.7–3.6 kg (6–8 lb) • COAT Thick, short and glossy • COLOUR Black and tan • LIFESPAN 12–13 years • ALSO KNOWN AS Manchester Terrier (Toy)

English Toy Terriers look like a smaller version of the Manchester Terrier, but have pricked ears. Cat-like and clean, they are active, lively and playful. Aloof with strangers, they prefer to be with their owners.

ORIGINALLY BRED to hunt and kill rats, later as a companion.

Special characteristics
This dog is alert, feisty and playful.

Exercise requirements
Medium. Needs to be kept entertained.

Attitude to
OWNERS affectionate, devoted
CHILDREN puppies and adults may be injured by boisterous children
OTHER PETS may be problematic with small pets
STRANGERS wary, aloof
UNFAMILIAR DOGS good if well socialized

Perfect owner
Gentle, playful experienced owner who can provide enough activity to keep this active dog entertained and who will enjoy its rather independent nature.

Potential problems
Tends to bark excessively. Lack of exercise may lead to escapes.

Toys

Griffon Bruxellois (Brussels Griffon)

lively • alert • good-natured • tenacious • courageous • sensitive

SIZE **18–20 cm (7–8 in)** • WEIGHT **2.3–5 kg (5–11 lb)** • COAT **Rough: harsh, wiry** • **Smooth: short and tight** • COLOUR **Clear red, black or black and rich tan without white markings** • LIFESPAN **12–14 years**

Toys

A possible descendant of the Affenpinscher, Griffon Bruxellois are lively and inquisitive. They have retained strong hunting instincts, make good watchdogs, are devoted to owners and friendly to strangers.

ORIGINALLY BRED to kill rats, later as a companion.

Special characteristics
Alert and active, the Griffon Bruxellois likes company.

Exercise requirements
Low. Enjoys exercise and play.

Attitude to
OWNERS affectionate, devoted
CHILDREN puppies and adults may be injured by boisterous children
OTHER PETS may be problematic with small pets
STRANGERS friendly if well socialized
UNFAMILIAR DOGS friendly if well socialized

Perfect owner
Gentle, sociable owner who will enjoy this playful, good-natured little dog.

Potential problems
May bark excessively.

⚠ This dog's bulbous eyes are prone to injury. Its shortened nose can make breathing difficult, and it is likely to snore. Some may be finicky eaters. Coat will need to be hand-stripped or clipped.

Havanese

lively • gentle • affectionate • responsive • friendly • sensitive • outgoing

SIZE **23–28 cm (9–11 in)** • WEIGHT **3–6 kg (7–13 lb)** • COAT **Soft, silky, wavy or slightly curled, full coated with an undercoat** • COLOUR **Any** • LIFESPAN **14 years**

Gentle and a little reserved with strangers, Havanese are responsive and devoted to their owners. Playful and outgoing, they are also sensitive and can be easily upset.

ORIGINALLY BRED to be a companion.

Special characteristics
The playful Havanese likes to be with people.

Exercise requirements
Medium. Enjoys playing.

Attitude to
OWNERS **affectionate, devoted**
CHILDREN **good**
OTHER PETS **good**
STRANGERS **reserved**
UNFAMILIAR DOGS **friendly**

Perfect owner
Gentle, affectionate owner who will enjoy grooming and playing with this sensitive, energetic little dog.

Potential problems
May suffer from separation problems.

Toys

⚠ The dog's full coat will bring in mud and dirt from outside, and requires daily brushing to prevent mats from forming. The long hair above the eyes needs to be clipped or tied up so that it can see clearly.

Italian Greyhound

elegant • affectionate • sweet-natured • sensitive • aloof

SIZE **32–38 cm (12½–15 in)** • WEIGHT **3.5–4.5 kg (8–10 lb)** • COAT **Short, fine and glossy. Can be cold in winter** • COLOUR **Black, blue, cream, fawn, red, white, or any of these colours broken with white** • LIFESPAN **14 years**

Toys

Elegant, sweet-natured and sensitive, Italian Greyhounds like to be close to their owners. Like their larger relations, they exercise in short bursts of lightning speed so safe areas are needed for walks.

ORIGINALLY BRED to be a companion.

Special characteristics
This dog likes to chase, and enjoys company.

Exercise requirements
Medium. Full of energy.

Attitude to
OWNERS **affectionate, devoted**
CHILDREN **good, but care needed with boisterous children**
OTHER PETS **good, may chase**
STRANGERS **reserved, discerning**
UNFAMILIAR DOGS **friendly if well socialized**

Perfect owner
Gentle, affectionate owner who can provide a safe area for this active dog to run off its energy.

Potential problems
May display control problems on walks. May be hard to housetrain.

Japanese Chin

happy • gentle • good-natured • delicate • independent

SIZE 23–25 cm (9–10 in) • WEIGHT 2–4 kg (4–8 lb) • COAT Profuse, long, soft, straight, of silky texture
• COLOUR Black and white or red and white • LIFESPAN 12–13 years

Japanese Chins are friendly, good-natured and make affectionate, devoted companions. They are playful and friendly to visitors. Their long coat needs regular grooming to keep it in good condition.

ORIGINALLY BRED to be a companion.

Special characteristics
This playful dog enjoys company.

Exercise requirements
Low. Content with short walks.

Attitude to
OWNERS affectionate, devoted
CHILDREN puppies and adults may be injured by boisterous children
OTHER PETS good
STRANGERS friendly
UNFAMILIAR DOGS friendly if well socialized

Perfect owner
Gentle, affectionate owner who will care for these delicate little dogs.

⚠️ The profuse coat will bring in mud and dirt from outside, and regular grooming is required to keep it in good condition. This dog's bulbous eyes are prone to injury. Its shortened nose can make breathing difficult, and it is likely to snore.

The shortened face and high brow gives these dogs a startled appearance.

Toys

King Charles Spaniel

happy • reserved • gentle • sensitive • affectionate

SIZE **25–27 cm (10–11 in)** • WEIGHT **4–6 kg (8–14 lb)** • COAT **Long, silky and straight** • COLOUR **Black and tan, tricolour, Blenheim (white with chestnut-red patches), ruby** • LIFESPAN **11–12 years** • ALSO KNOWN AS **English Toy Terrier**

Toys

Smaller and less popular than the Cavalier, the King Charles Spaniel has a shorter face and is less friendly to strangers. They are happy and devoted to owners, but reserved with people outside the family.

ORIGINALLY BRED **to be a companion.**

Special characteristics
This is a playful dog that likes human company.

Exercise requirements
Low. Does not need too much in the way of exercise.

Attitude to
OWNERS **affectionate, devoted**
CHILDREN **puppies and adults may be injured by boisterous children**
OTHER PETS **good**
STRANGERS **reserved**
UNFAMILIAR DOGS **friendly**

Perfect owner
Affectionate, gentle owner who lives a quiet life.

⚠ This dog's shortened nose can make breathing difficult, and it is likely to snore.

Lowchen

happy • lively • independent • strong-willed • stubborn

SIZE **25–33 cm (10–13 in)** • WEIGHT **4–8 kg (9–18 lb)** • COAT **Fairly long single coat of soft texture** • COLOUR **Any** • LIFESPAN **13–14 years** • In the 'Non-sporting' class in the USA

Show owners shave off the coat on the hind legs to make Lowchens resemble small lions. In character, they are wilful and stubborn. They are affectionate but independent with owners, and are only friendly to strangers and other dogs if well socialized when young.

ORIGINALLY BRED as a companion.

Special characteristics
This playful dog likes company.

Exercise requirements
Low. Enjoys play.

Attitude to
OWNERS affectionate, independent
CHILDREN good
OTHER PETS good, can be problematic with other dogs in the family
STRANGERS friendly if well socialized
UNFAMILIAR DOGS can be problematic

Perfect owner
Affectionate, confident owner who will enjoy playing with and training this small dog with an independent spirit.

Potential problems
May display status-related problems with gentle owners.

⚠️ The hair on the top of the head may need to be clipped or tied up so that the dog can see clearly.

Toys

Maltese

lively • alert • sweet-tempered • affectionate

SIZE **20–25 cm (8–10 in)** • WEIGHT **2–3 kg (4–6 lb)** • COAT **Long, straight, of silky texture** • COLOUR **White**
• LIFESPAN **14 years**

Toys

Lively, gentle and sweet-natured Maltese look very much like toys with their snow white hair tied up with a ribbon on top of their heads. They are happy and friendly to all, and affectionate and devoted to owners. Daily grooming of the coat is essential.

ORIGINALLY BRED as a companion.

Special characteristics
The playful Maltese enjoys company.

Exercise requirements
Medium. Loves exercise.

Attitude to
OWNERS **affectionate, devoted**
CHILDREN **good**
OTHER PETS **good**
STRANGERS **friendly**
UNFAMILIAR DOGS **friendly**

Perfect owner
Affectionate, playful, gentle owner with plenty of time for grooming.

⚠ The long, silky hair will bring in mud and dirt from outside, and the coat needs daily grooming or regular clipping to prevent mats from forming.

The hair on the head of the Maltese needs to be tied up out of the eyes.

Miniature Pinscher

confident • spirited • courageous • feisty • alert • lively • curious

SIZE 25–30 cm (10–12 in) • WEIGHT 4–5 kg (8–10 lb) • COAT Smooth, hard and short • COLOUR Black, blue, chocolate with sharply defined tan markings or solid red • LIFESPAN 13–14 years

Miniature Pinschers have a distinctive gait, flexing at the knees more than other dogs. They are spirited and lively, with terrier-like instincts for hunting and a playful, feisty nature. Curious and independent, they are constantly busy and active.

ORIGINALLY BRED to hunt rats and then as a companion.

Special characteristics
This alert dog enjoys company and has a playful nature.

Exercise requirements
Medium. Busy at home and outside.

Attitude to
OWNERS affectionate, independent
CHILDREN puppies and adults may be injured by boisterous children
OTHER PETS may be problematic with small pets
STRANGERS friendly if well socialized
UNFAMILIAR DOGS friendly if well socialized

Perfect owner
Active, affectionate, confident owner who will enjoy finding safe places to exercise and play with this active, independent little dog.

Potential problems
May try to escape if bored.

Papillon

lively • friendly • alert • biddable

SIZE **20–28 cm (8–11 in)** • WEIGHT **4–4.5 kg (9–10 lb)** • COAT **Long, fine, silky, without undercoat** • COLOUR **White with patches, or tricolour** • LIFESPAN **14 years**

Toys

Papillons get their name from their dramatic ears, reminiscent of butterflies' wings. They are lively, responsive and devoted to their owners and can be wary of strangers and other dogs unless they are socialized well and early.

ORIGINALLY BRED as a companion.

Special characteristics
Alert and playful, the Papillon enjoys company.

Exercise requirements
Medium. Busy at home and outside.

Attitude to
OWNERS **affectionate, devoted**
CHILDREN **puppies and adults may be injured by young or boisterous children**
OTHER PETS **good**
STRANGERS **wary unless well socialized**
UNFAMILIAR DOGS **good if well socialized**

Perfect owner
Gentle, affectionate owner who will enjoy playing with, exercising and training this energetic little dog.

Potential problems
Tends to bark excessively. Some suffer from separation problems.

⚠ The silky coat requires daily grooming to prevent mats from forming.

Pekingese

alert • courageous • loyal • calm • aloof • independent • stubborn

SIZE 15–23 cm (6–9 in) • WEIGHT 4–5.5 kg (10–12 lb) • COAT Long, straight with profuse mane and thick undercoat. Profuse feathering on ears, back of legs, tail and toes • COLOUR All colours • LIFESPAN 12–13 years

Toys

Pekingese were bred by ancient Chinese Royal Courts to have short, bowed legs so they could not wander far. Added to this they have a very thick coat making them prone to overheating and a shortened nose making breathing difficult so they do not enjoy exercise. Pekingese can be stubborn, aloof and independent.

ORIGINALLY BRED as a companion.

Special characteristics
The Pekingese is an alert dog that enjoys company.

Exercise requirements
Low. The thick coat and breathing difficulties caused by its short nose sap its energy.

Attitude to
OWNERS affectionate, loyal
CHILDREN puppies and adults may be injured by young or boisterous children
OTHER PETS good
STRANGERS aloof
UNFAMILIAR DOGS good if well socialized

Perfect owner
Easy-going, gentle owner who will enjoy grooming and petting this independent little dog.

Potential problems
Tends to bark excessively.

⚠ This dog's long coat will bring in mud and dirt from outside, and requires daily grooming to prevent mats from forming. Its bulbous eyes are prone to injury, and the shortened nose can make breathing difficult, so it is likely to snore.

Pomeranian

vivacious • extrovert • lively • affectionate

SIZE 22–28 cm (8½–11 in) • WEIGHT 1.8–2.5 kg (4–5½ lb) • COAT Long, straight, harsh topcoat, with soft, fluffy undercoat • COLOUR Any • LIFESPAN 15 years

Toys

Pomeranians are lively, busy and extrovert. They are affectionate and devoted to their owners and are alert watchdogs, although early control is needed to prevent barking becoming excessive. Their coat is thick and needs daily care.

ORIGINALLY BRED to be a companion.

⚠ This dog's long coat will bring mud and dirt in from outside, and requires daily grooming to prevent mats from forming.

The head of the Pomeranian resembles a small ball.

Special characteristics
The Pomeranian is alert and enjoys company.

Exercise requirements
Medium. Busy at home and outside.

Attitude to
OWNERS affectionate, devoted
CHILDREN puppies and adults may be injured by boisterous children
OTHER PETS good
STRANGERS good if well socialized
UNFAMILIAR DOGS good if well socialized

Perfect owner
Active, gentle, affectionate owner with time to groom and play.

Potential problems
Tends to bark excessively.

Pug

homely • friendly • industrious • sociable • gentle • playful • obedient • busy

SIZE 25–28 cm (10–11 in) • WEIGHT 6.5–8 kg (14–18 lb) • COAT Fine, soft, short and glossy • COLOUR Silver, apricot, fawn or black. Muzzle or mask, ears, moles on cheeks, thumb mark or diamond on forehead and trace as black as possible • LIFESPAN 13–14 years

Independent, wilful and resolute, Pugs are forceful and determined. Distinctive and endearing, they are loyal, playful companions.

ORIGINALLY BRED to be a companion.

Special characteristics
Alert and playful, the Pug enjoys company.

Exercise requirements
Low. Stocky but can move fast.

Attitude to
OWNERS affectionate, loyal
CHILDREN puppies and adults may be injured by boisterous children
OTHER PETS good
STRANGERS friendly
UNFAMILIAR DOGS friendly

Perfect owner
Affectionate, gentle owner who will enjoy this friendly, independent little character.

⚠️ This dog's bulbous eyes are prone to injury. Its shortened nose can make breathing difficult, and it is likely to snore.

Toys

Toy Fox Terrier (American Toy Terrier)

bright • alert • courageous • playful • energetic • independent

SIZE **24.5–25.5 cm (10 in)** • WEIGHT **2–3 kg (4½–7 lb)** • COAT Smooth, short • COLOUR Tricolour, tan and white, black and white • LIFESPAN 13–14 years

Toys

Energetic and alert, Toy Fox Terriers are quick, energetic and playful. They like to be busy and are determined little hunters given the chance. Friendly and affectionate, they are easily aroused and need plenty of early socialization to keep them tolerant of others.

ORIGINALLY BRED to hunt rats, then as a companion.

Special characteristics
The Toy Fox Terrier is alert and playful, and likes company.

Exercise requirements
Medium. Busy at home and outside.

Attitude to
OWNERS affectionate, devoted
CHILDREN puppies and adults may be injured by boisterous children
OTHER PETS may be problematic with small pets
STRANGERS good if well socialized
UNFAMILIAR DOGS good if well socialized

Perfect owner
Active, affectionate owner who will enjoy exercising, playing with and training this lively, independent little dog.

Yorkshire Terrier

alert • spirited • friendly • courageous • tenacious • stubborn

SIZE **22.5–23.5 cm (9 in)** • WEIGHT **2.5–3.5 kg (5–7 lb)** • COAT **Long, straight, fine, silky texture** • COLOUR **Dark steel blue and bright tan** • LIFESPAN **14 years**

Bred by miners to hunt rats, Yorkshire Terriers are feisty, courageous hunters despite their small size. Playful, tenacious and stubborn, these busy little dogs make good watchdogs. Excessive barking will need to be controlled and they require daily grooming sessions to de-tangle their long hair.

ORIGINALLY BRED **to hunt and kill rats.**

Special characteristics
The Yorkshire Terrier is alert, playful and feisty.

Exercise requirements
High. Busy at home and outside.

Attitude to
OWNERS **affectionate, loyal**
CHILDREN **puppies and adults may be injured by boisterous children**
OTHER PETS **may kill small pets, may injure cats unless raised with them**
STRANGERS **good if well socialized**
UNFAMILIAR DOGS **good if well socialized**

Perfect owner
Active, affectionate, gentle owner who can provide plenty of exercise and play for this lively little dog.

Potential problems
Tends to bark excessively, especially if under-exercised.

⚠ This dog's coat will bring mud and dirt in from outdoors, and requires daily grooming to prevent mats from forming. The long hair on the top of the head needs to be clipped or tied up out of the eyes so the dog can see clearly.

Akita

dignified • courageous • aloof • calm • independent • undemonstrative • stubborn

SIZE 61–71 cm (24–28 in) • WEIGHT 34–50 kg (75–110 lb) • COAT Medium length, coarse, straight topcoat with soft, dense undercoat • COLOUR Any • LIFESPAN 10–12 years • In the 'Working' class in the USA

Utility

Independent and aloof, Akitas are slow to show their feelings. They are reserved with strangers and need appropriate and continued socialization with people and other dogs to stay tolerant. Powerful, courageous and determined, they are best suited to experienced, strong-willed owners.

ORIGINALLY BRED to hunt large game, guard, and fight other dogs.

Perfect owner
Experienced, strong-willed, independent owner who can provide plenty of socialization, safe exercise and plenty of games and activity.

Potential problems
May to be aggressive to other dogs, and may display status-related aggression to gentle owners.

Special characteristics
The Akita is determined, with a powerful, muscular build.

Exercise requirements
Medium. Enjoys exercise.

Attitude to
OWNERS loyal, independent
CHILDREN natural guard, not tolerant
OTHER PETS will kill small animals, will chase
STRANGERS reserved, territorial
UNFAMILIAR DOGS can be problematic/aggressive unless well socialized

American Eskimo Dog

alert • active • courageous • independent • affectionate

SIZE Toy: 23–30cm (9–12 in) • Miniature: 33–38 cm (12–15 in) • Standard: over 38 cm (over 15 in)
• WEIGHT Toy: 2.5–4.5 kg (6–10 lb) • Miniature: 4.5–9 kg (10–20 lb) • Standard: 9–16 kg (20–35 lb)
• COAT Profuse, long with dense undercoat • COLOUR White • lifespan 12–13 years

American Eskimo Dogs come in three sizes. Alert and active, they make good watchdogs. They can be wary and shy with strangers and are loyal and independent with owners.

ORIGINALLY BRED to be a companion.

Special characteristics
This lively and playful dog enjoys company.

Exercise requirements
High. Plenty of stamina.

Attitude to
OWNERS affectionate, loyal
CHILDREN good if raised with them
OTHER PETS good if raised with them
STRANGERS wary unless well socialized
UNFAMILIAR DOGS good if well socialized

Perfect owner
Active, patient, calm owner who has plenty of time for grooming, play and activity.

Potential problems
Tends to bark excessively. May be hard to housetrain and may chew if bored.

⚠ This dog's coat will bring in mud and dirt from outside, and daily brushing is needed to prevent mats from forming. The thick coat also means that the owner should ensure the dog does not overheat in summer.

Utility

Boston Terrier

lively • determined • considerate • sensible • good-natured • outgoing

SIZE **38–43 cm (15–17 in)** • WEIGHT **6.8–11.5 kg (15–25 lb)** • COAT **Short, smooth, fine** • COLOUR **Brindle with white markings, black with white markings** • LIFESPAN **13 years**

Utility

Very unlike other terriers in nature, the Boston Terrier would rather be with people than out hunting and getting into mischief. Sensible and considerate, they make friendly, good-natured pets.

ORIGINALLY BRED as a companion.

Special characteristics
Alert and playful, the Boston Terrier enjoys company.

Exercise requirements
Medium. Undemanding.

Attitude to
OWNERS affectionate, loyal
CHILDREN good
OTHER PETS usually good
STRANGERS friendly if socialized
UNFAMILIAR DOGS friendly if socialized

Perfect owner
Gentle, good-natured owner who enjoys playing and socializing.

⚠ This dog's bulbous eyes are prone to injury. Its shortened nose can make breathing difficult, and it is likely to snore. Bitches may have trouble giving birth naturally due to the large heads of their puppies.

Bulldog

kind • courageous • tenacious • alert • bold • affectionate • stubborn

SIZE **31–36 cm (12–14 in)** • WEIGHT **23–25 kg (50–55 lb)** • COAT **Fine, short, close, smooth** • COLOUR **Whole colours or whole colours with white** • LIFESPAN **8–9 years**

Affectionate, resolute and courageous, Bulldogs are devoted to their owners. They are sociable with strangers, but they need careful socializing to be tolerant of other dogs. The design of their bodies causes them many difficulties and they are not very active or lively as a result.

ORIGINALLY BRED for bull-and bear-baiting and dog-fighting.

Special characteristics
The Bulldog is alert and friendly.

Exercise requirements
Low. Restricted breathing and an ungainly body sap energy.

Attitude to
OWNERS **affectionate, devoted**
CHILDREN **good**
OTHER PETS **good**
STRANGERS **friendly**
UNFAMILIAR DOGS **can be problematic**

Perfect owner
Affectionate, tolerant owner who will enjoy this characterful but slow companion.

Potential problems
Tends to be aggressive to other dogs if provoked.

The shortened face results in an undershot jaw leaving the bottom teeth sticking out below the top teeth.

⚠ The folds of skin above the nose and around the tail need regular cleaning. This dog's shortened muzzle may cause lack of saliva control, and can make breathing difficult, especially in hot weather. It is likely to snore. Bitches cannot give birth naturally due to the puppies' large heads, so a Caesarean section is necessary.

Utility

Canaan Dog

agile • alert • confident • vigilant • aloof with strangers

SIZE **50–60 cm (20–24 in)** • WEIGHT **18–25 kg (40–55 lb)** • COAT Outer coat dense, harsh, straight, of short to medium length with close profuse undercoat • COLOUR Sand to red-brown, white, black, or spotted, with or without a symmetrical black mask • LIFESPAN 12–13 years • In the 'Herding' class in the USA

Utility

Canaan Dogs are alert, and make good watchdogs. With owners, they are aloof but responsive and willing to please. They are quick and able hunters, and do not find it easy to get on with strangers or other dogs.

ORIGINALLY BRED to herd, guard, and track.

Special characteristics
The Canaan dog is alert, agile and curious.

Exercise requirements
Medium. Enjoys plenty of exercise.

Attitude to
OWNERS aloof, responsive
CHILDREN good if raised with them
OTHER PETS may be problematic with small pets, may chase cats
STRANGERS aloof, wary
UNFAMILIAR DOGS can be problematic/aggressive

Perfect owner
Experienced, active, independent owner who has plenty of time for exercise, training and play.

Potential problems
Tends to be aggressive to other dogs.

Chow Chow

aloof • independent • stubborn • strong-willed • quiet • good guard • loyal

SIZE 46–56 cm (18–22 in) • WEIGHT 20–32 kg (45–70 lb) • COAT Rough: Profuse, abundant, dense, straight with soft, woolly undercoat • Smooth: Short, abundant, dense, straight • COLOUR Red, black, cream, blue and cinnamon. Tongue is blue-black • LIFESPAN 11–12 years

With its unusual blue-black tongue, the Chow Chow is a dog for the enthusiast. Independent, stubborn and reserved, they are not very tolerant or playful and will resist being handled unless they are used to it from a very early age. Their thick coat makes it likely that they will overheat on hot days, adding to their intolerance of others.

ORIGINALLY BRED to hunt, herd, guard, pull sleds, also used for their meat and fur.

Special characteristics
The Chow Chow is quiet and independent, not a playful dog.

Chow Chows have a distinctive blue/black tongue.

Exercise requirements
Low.

Attitude to
OWNERS aloof, independent
CHILDREN not very sociable, intolerant, not playful
OTHER PETS may be problematic
STRANGERS suspicious and territorial
UNFAMILIAR DOGS can be problematic

Perfect owner
Confident, experienced owner who likes their dog to be independent, no trouble and without much interaction or strong desire to please.

Potential problems
Prone to overheating and can be irritable on hot days. May be controlling or intolerant of handling, particularly by strangers. May guard food and possessions.

Utility

Dalmatian

great endurance • outgoing • friendly • exuberant

SIZE **56–61 cm (22–24 in)** • WEIGHT **23–25 kg (50–55 lb)** • COAT **Short, hard, sleek** • COLOUR **Ground colour pure white. Black-spotted, dense black spots, and liver-spotted, liver-brown spots** • LIFESPAN **12 years**

Utility

Distinctive, elegant, exuberant and agile, Dalmatians like to run and run. They are enjoyable pets providing they can get the exercise they need, and are friendly and affectionate. Good socialization is needed from an early age to ensure tolerance of other dogs.

ORIGINALLY BRED to run alongside carriages.

Special characteristics
The Dalmation loves running, and has plenty of stamina.

Exercise requirements
High. Quiet at home but needs long, energetic walks.

Attitude to
OWNERS **affectionate, devoted**
CHILDREN **good if raised with them**
OTHER PETS **good, may chase**
STRANGERS **friendly if socialized**
UNFAMILIAR DOGS **can be problematic**

Perfect owner
Active, energetic owner who will enjoy long walks with this dog.

Potential problems
May display control problems on a walk, escaping if under-exercised.

French Bulldog

courageous • vivacious • affectionate • responsive

SIZE 30–31 cm (12 in) • WEIGHT 11–12.5 kg (24–28 lb) • COAT Fine, smooth, short • COLOUR Brindle, pied or fawn • LIFESPAN 11–12 years

Lively and affectionate, French Bulldogs are sweet-natured and make good companions. They are playful and alert and do not require too much exercise. Good socialization is needed with other dogs early on to ensure they are friendly with them later.

ORIGINALLY BRED as a companion (from bull-baiting stock).

Special characteristics
This dog is alert, friendly and playful.

Exercise requirements
Low. Finds hot days hard going.

Attitude to
OWNERS affectionate, devoted
CHILDREN good if raised with them
OTHER PETS good
STRANGERS friendly
UNFAMILIAR DOGS friendly if well socialized

Perfect owner
Affectionate, sociable owner who will enjoy this sweet-natured little dog.

Utility

⚠ This dog's shortened nose can make breathing difficult, especially in hot weather, and it is likely to snore. The wrinkles on the face need to be cleaned daily.

German Spitz

German Spitz come in the Klein (Toy) and Mittel (Standard) varieties (there is also a giant variety too). All are feisty, and reactive. Their profuse coat requires daily care and they may be intolerant of this unless handled carefully. Potentially problematic with strangers and other dogs, they make good watchdogs.

Utility

Klein

active • alert • independent • confident • curious • bold

SIZE 23–29 cm (9–11½ in) • WEIGHT 8–10 kg (18–22 lb) • COAT Long, harsh topcoat with soft woolly undercoat. Very abundant around neck and forequarters • COLOUR Any • LIFESPAN 14–15 years

ORIGINALLY BRED to be a watchdog and companion.

Special characteristics
The German Spitz is alert, reactive and lively.

Exercise requirements
Medium.

Attitude to
OWNERS affectionate, loyal
CHILDREN puppies and adults may be injured by young or boisterous children
OTHER PETS may be problematic
STRANGERS reserved, territorial unless well socialized
UNFAMILIAR DOGS can be problematic unless well socialized

Perfect owner
Experienced, active owner who has plenty of time for grooming, play and exercise.

Potential problems
May bark excessively.

Mittel

active • alert • independent • confident • curious • bold

SIZE 30–38 cm (12–15 in) • WEIGHT 10.5–11.5 kg (23–41 lb) • COAT Long, harsh topcoat with soft woolly undercoat. Very abundant around neck and forequarters • COLOUR Any • LIFESPAN 13–14 years

ORIGINALLY BRED to work on farms, then as a companion.

Special characteristics
The German Spitz is alert, reactive and lively.

Exercise requirements
Medium.

Attitude to
OWNERS affectionate, loyal
CHILDREN puppies and adults may be injured by boisterous children
OTHER PETS may be problematic
STRANGERS reserved, territorial unless well socialized
UNFAMILIAR DOGS can be problematic unless well socialized

Perfect owner
Experienced, active owner who has plenty of time for grooming, play and exercise.

Potential problems
May bark excessively.

Utility

⚠ The long coat will bring in mud and dirt from outside and needs daily grooming to prevent mats from forming.

Japanese Shiba Inu

confident • lively • friendly • quiet • independent • spirited

SIZE 36.5–39.5 cm (14½–15½ in) • WEIGHT 8–10 kg (18–22 lb) • COAT Hard, straight outer coat with soft, dense undercoat • COLOUR Red, red sesame, black and tan, white • LIFESPAN 12–13 years

Utility

Aloof and independent, Japanese Shiba Inus are reluctant to show their feelings. They are quiet and rarely bark, and can be reserved with strangers and problematic with other dogs unless they have been well socialized. With their owners, they are playful and enjoy company.

ORIGINALLY BRED to hunt small game, then as a companion.

Special characteristics
This dog is alert and playful, and enjoys company.

Exercise requirements
Medium. Likes joining in activities.

Attitude to
OWNERS affectionate, aloof
CHILDREN good if raised with them
OTHER PETS good if raised
with them
STRANGERS reserved, aloof
UNFAMILIAR DOGS can be
problematic

Perfect owner
Experienced, strong-willed owner who will enjoy training, socializing and playing.

Potential problems
May display status-related aggression with gentle owners, and tends to be aggressive to other dogs.

Japanese Spitz

affectionate • aloof with strangers • alert • bold • lively • independent

SIZE **30–36 cm (12–14 in)** • WEIGHT **5–6 kg (11–13 lb)** • COAT **Straight topcoat with profuse, short, dense undercoat** • COLOUR **White** • LIFESPAN **12 years**

Lively and bold, Japanese Spitz make good watchdogs. They are affectionate and loyal to owners, but tend to be reserved with strangers.

ORIGINALLY BRED as a companion.

⚠ This dog's coat will bring mud and dirt into the house and needs daily grooming to prevent mats from forming.

Special characteristics
The Japanese Spitz is alert and playful, and enjoys company.

Exercise requirements
Medium. Busy in the house and outside.

Attitude to
OWNERS affectionate, loyal
CHILDREN good if raised with them
OTHER PETS good if raised with them
STRANGERS wary, reserved
UNFAMILIAR DOGS good if well socialized

Perfect owner
Active, affectionate owner who has plenty of time for grooming, exercising, playing and training.

Potential problems
Tends to bark excessively.

Utility

Keeshond

sturdy • sensible • good-natured • adaptable • bold • alert • friendly

SIZE **43–46 cm (17–18 in)** • WEIGHT **25–30 kg (55–66 lb)** • COAT **Harsh, straight topcoat with soft, thick undercoat** • COLOUR **Mixture of grey and black** • LIFESPAN **12–14 years**

Utility

Keeshonds are alert and vocal and make good watchdogs. They are friendly, busy and adaptable and make good-natured companions if well socialized and exercised. Their thick coats require daily attention.

ORIGINALLY BRED as a watchdog for farms and barges.

Special characteristics
The Keeshond is alert, vocal and excitable.

Exercise requirements
Medium. Busy at home and outside.

Attitude to
OWNERS affectionate, loyal
CHILDREN good if raised with them
OTHER PETS good if raised with them
STRANGERS friendly if socialized
UNFAMILIAR DOGS friendly if socialized

⚠ This dog's coat will bring mud and dirt in from outside and needs daily grooming to prevent mats from forming.

Perfect owner
Active, affectionate owner who has plenty of time for grooming, games and exercise.

Potential problems
Tends to bark excessively.

Lhasa Apso

assertive • alert • steady • confident • aloof with strangers • stubborn

SIZE 25–28 cm (10–11 in) • WEIGHT 6–7 kg (13–15 lb) • COAT Topcoat long, heavy, straight, hard with moderate undercoat • COLOUR Golden, sandy, honey, dark grizzle, slate, smoke, particolour, black, white or brown • LIFESPAN 12–14 years

Lhasa Apsos originated in Tibet and are alert and reserved with strangers. They make good watchdogs, but their tendency to bark needs to be controlled. Their coat needs daily care and early handling is advisable as their tolerance for interference is low. Early socialization is needed for them to be tolerant of other dogs.

ORIGINALLY BRED to be companions for monks.

Special characteristics
The Lhasa Apso is an alert and vocal dog.

Exercise requirements
Medium. Will cheerfully walk long distances.

Attitude to
OWNERS affectionate, loyal
CHILDREN good if raised with them
OTHER PETS good if raised with them
STRANGERS aloof, reserved
UNFAMILIAR DOGS can be problematic

Perfect owner
Experienced, tolerant owner who has time for grooming and continued socialization and training with their pet.

Potential problems
Tends to bark excessively. May be aggressive with gentle owners to get its own way.

⚠ The long coat needs daily brushing to prevent mats from forming. Owners may prefer to have the coat clipped regularly. The hair needs to be trimmed or tied up out of the eyes so that the dog can see clearly.

Utility

Schnauzers

Lively and terrier-like, Schnauzers are inquisitive and persistent. They are friendly and playful, and responsive and affectionate to owners. Barking is a favourite hobby and they make excellent watchdogs.

Miniature

alert • reliable • biddable • inquisitive • eager • persistent

SIZE 33–36 cm (13–14 in) • WEIGHT 6–7 kg (13–15 lb) • COAT Harsh, wiry with dense undercoat • COLOUR All pepper and salt colours • LIFESPAN 14 years • In the 'Terrier' class in the USA

ORIGINALLY BRED to hunt rats, then as a companion.

Special characteristics
Alert and playful, the Schnauzer enjoys company.

Exercise requirements
Medium. Busy at home and outside.

Attitude to
OWNERS affectionate, loyal
CHILDREN good when raised with them
OTHER PETS good when raised with them
STRANGERS friendly if well socialized
UNFAMILIAR DOGS friendly if well socialized

Perfect owner
Active, confident, affectionate owner who enjoys playing, training and grooming.

Potential problems
Tends to bark excessively.

Standard

alert • reliable • calm • biddable • inquisitive • eager • persistent

SIZE 46–48 cm (18–19 in) • WEIGHT 14.5–15.5 kg (32–34 lb) • COAT Harsh, wiry with dense undercoat
• COLOUR Pure black or pepper and salt • LIFESPAN 12–14 years • In the 'Working' class in the USA

ORIGINALLY BRED to hunt rats and to guard, later as a companion.

Special characteristics
Alert and playful, the Schnauzer enjoys company.

Exercise requirements
Medium. Busy at home and outside.

Attitude to
OWNERS affectionate, loyal
CHILDREN good when raised with them
OTHER PETS good when raised with them
STRANGERS friendly if well socialized, territorial
UNFAMILIAR DOGS friendly if well socialized

Perfect owner
Active, confident, affectionate owner who enjoys playing, training and grooming.

Potential problems
Tends to bark excessively.

Utility

⚠ The wiry coat needs daily brushing to keep it tangle-free, and regular clipping.

Poodles

Poodles come in three varieties, Toy (small), Miniature (medium), and Standard (large). Lively, spirited and responsive, they are easily trained and reliable companions. Although their show clips can make them look frivolous, they are serious, willing and good-natured workers and make excellent companions for active owners. Their coat needs to be clipped regularly. (The show clip is an exaggeration of a clip designed to protect joints in cold water. Pet owners, and dog, may prefer the all-over puppy clips instead).

Miniature

spirited • good-natured • biddable • affectionate • calm • dependable

SIZE 28–38 cm (11–15 in) (larger than the Toy Poodle) • WEIGHT 12–14 kg (26–30 lb) • COAT Very profuse and dense. Does not shed • COLOUR All solid colours • LIFESPAN 14–15 years

ORIGINALLY BRED as a companion.

Special characteristics
Alert and playful, this poodle
enjoys company.

Exercise requirements
Medium.

Attitude to
OWNERS affectionate, responsive
CHILDREN good
OTHER PETS good
STRANGERS friendly if socialized
UNFAMILIAR DOGS friendly if socialized

Perfect owner
Active, affectionate owner who will
enjoy grooming, exercising, playing
and training this dynamic little dog.

Utility

Standard

spirited • good-natured • biddable • affectionate • calm • dependable

SIZE **37.5–38.5 cm (15 in)** • WEIGHT **20.5–32 kg (45–70 lb)** • COAT **Very profuse and dense. Does not shed** • COLOUR **All solid colours** • LIFESPAN **11–13 years**

ORIGINALLY BRED to retrieve birds from water.

Special characteristics
Lively and playful, this poodle loves people.

Exercise requirements
High. Enjoys racing about.

Attitude to
OWNERS **affectionate, responsive**
CHILDREN **good**
OTHER PETS **good**
STRANGERS **friendly**
UNFAMILIAR DOGS **friendly**

Perfect owner
Active, affectionate owner who enjoys energetic walks, grooming, training and playing.

Utility

✔ Recommended for first-time owners especially if they are prone to allergies. Care is needed to find a healthy dog free of inherited disease.

Toy

spirited • good-natured • biddable • affectionate • calm • dependable

SIZE **25–28 cm (10–11 in)** • WEIGHT **6.5–7.5 kg (14–16½ lb)** • COAT **Very profuse and dense. Does not shed** • COLOUR **All solid colours** • LIFESPAN **14–15 years**

Utility

ORIGINALLY BRED as a companion.

Special characteristics
This poodle is alert and playful, and enjoys company.

Exercise requirements
Medium.

Attitude to
OWNERS **affectionate, responsive**
CHILDREN **puppies and adults may be injured by boisterous children**
OTHER PETS **good**
STRANGERS **friendly if socialized**
UNFAMILIAR DOGS **friendly if socialized**

Perfect owner
Active, affectionate owner who will enjoy grooming, exercising, playing and training this dynamic little dog.

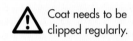 Coat needs to be clipped regularly.

Schipperke

lively • alert • amenable • responsive • loyal • inquisitive

SIZE 22–33 cm (9–13 in) • WEIGHT 5.5–7.5 kg (12–16 lb) • COAT Abundant, dense and harsh
• COLOUR Usually black, but other whole colours permissible • LIFESPAN 12–13 years

Schipperkes are loyal and affectionate to owners, but wary of strangers. Their love of barking makes them excellent watchdogs, but this trait needs to be controlled if it not to become excessive. Alert, busy and inquisitive, they need plenty of socialization with other dogs to remain tolerant.

ORIGINALLY BRED as a watchdog on barges, later as a companion.

Special characteristics
The Schipperke is an alert, watchful and playful dog.

Exercise requirements
High. Busy at home and outside.

Attitude to
OWNERS affectionate, loyal
CHILDREN good if raised with them
OTHER PETS may be problematic with small pets
STRANGERS wary, territorial
UNFAMILIAR DOGS can be problematic

Perfect owner
Active, affectionate owner who enjoys grooming and who can provide plenty of activity, exercise and training.

Potential problems
Tends to bark excessively. May be difficult to housetrain.

Utility

⚠ The dense coat needs regular grooming to keep it in good condition.

Shar Pei

calm • independent • affectionate • wilful • aloof

SIZE 46–51cm (18–20 in) • WEIGHT 16–20 kg (35–45 lb) • COAT Harsh with no undercoat • COLOUR Any solid colours • LIFESPAN 11–12 years • ALSO KNOWN AS Chinese Shar Pei

Utility

Covered in distinctive folds of loose skin, many individuals of this breed pay the price for the fashionable excess of skin with painful eye problems and skin conditions. Good-natured and wilful, Shar Peis are independent and aloof and require early socialization to be tolerant of other dogs.

ORIGINALLY BRED for dog-fighting and hunting.

Special characteristics
The Shar Pei is courageous and tenacious.

The excessive wrinkles can cause painful eye conditions. Daily cleaning of the deep skin is essential to keep the coat in good condition.

Exercise requirements
Medium.

Attitude to
OWNERS affectionate, aloof
CHILDREN good if raised with them
OTHER PETS may be problematic with small pets
STRANGERS friendly if well socialized
UNFAMILIAR DOGS can be problematic

Perfect owner
Strong-willed, confident, affectionate owner who has plenty of time to care for and socialize this dog.

⚠ Take care to find a healthy line whose dogs have not had to have their eyelids surgically altered.

Shih Tzu

active • alert • friendly • independent

SIZE **25–27 cm (10–11 in)** • WEIGHT **4.5–7.5 kg (10–16 lb)** • COAT **Long, dense topcoat with good undercoat** • COLOUR **Any** • LIFESPAN **12–14 years** • **In the 'Toy' class in the USA**

Easily confused with the Lhasa Apso due to the similar appearance, Shih Tzus have a shortened face and a more amenable disposition. They are friendly with everyone if well socialized, and playful and devoted to their owners.

ORIGINALLY BRED as a companion.

Special characteristics
Alert and playful, the Shih Tzu enjoys company.

Exercise requirements
Low.

Attitude to
OWNERS **affectionate, devoted**
CHILDREN **good if raised with them**
OTHER PETS **good if raised with them**
STRANGERS **friendly if well socialized**
UNFAMILIAR DOGS **friendly if well socialized**

Perfect owner
Active, sensible, affectionate owner who enjoys grooming, playing and socializing their pet.

⚠ The dog's coat will bring in mud and dirt from outside and requires daily grooming to prevent mats from forming. The hair on the head should be clipped or tied up out of the eyes so that the dog can see clearly. The bulbous eyes are easily injured. The shortened muzzle can make breathing difficult, and it is likely to snore.

Utility

Tibetan Spaniel

assertive • playful • alert • loyal • confident • independent

SIZE **24–25 cm (9–10 in)** • WEIGHT **4–7 kg (9–15 lb)** • COAT **Silky topcoat, with fine, dense undercoat** • COLOUR **Any** • LIFESPAN **13–14 years**

Utility

Tibetan Spaniels are unlikely to have been used for hunting as the name implies, but instead are probably related to Pekingeses. Playful, lively and independent, they make good-natured pets. They are very vocal and this tendency needs to be controlled to prevent problems with excessive barking.

ORIGINALLY BRED as a watchdog and companion for monks in Tibet.

Special characteristics
The Tibetan Spaniel is alert, curious and vocal.

Exercise requirements
Medium. Enjoys rushing around the garden or yard.

Attitude to
OWNERS **affectionate, loyal**
CHILDREN **puppies and adults may be injured by boisterous children**
OTHER PETS **good**
STRANGERS **friendly, will bark**
UNFAMILIAR DOGS **friendly**

Perfect owner
Active, sociable owner who enjoys energetic walks and playing games.

Potential problems
Tends to bark excessively.

⚠ The bulbous eyes are easily injured. The dog's coat will bring in mud and dirt from outside, and daily grooming is required to prevent mats from forming.

Tibetan Terrier

lively • loyal • outgoing • alert • aloof with strangers • persistent

SIZE **36–41 cm (14–16 in)** • WEIGHT **8–14 kg (18–30 lb)** • COAT **Profuse, fine topcoat with fine, woolly undercoat** • COLOUR **Any except chocolate or liver** • LIFESPAN **13–14 years**

A terrier in name only, this breed is lively, outgoing and affectionate with owners. They are reserved and aloof with strangers and make good watchdogs, although owners need to be careful about excessive barking.

ORIGINALLY BRED to guard Tibetan monasteries and as a companion.

Special characteristics
This dog is alert, vocal and protective.

Exercise requirements
Medium. Nimble and energetic.

Attitude to
OWNERS affectionate, loyal
CHILDREN good if raised with them
OTHER PETS good if raised with them
STRANGERS aloof, reserved
UNFAMILIAR DOGS okay if well socialized

Perfect owner
Experienced, strong-willed, active owner who enjoys grooming and has time for plenty of play, training and activity.

Potential problems
May bark excessively.

⚠ The dog's coat will bring in mud and dirt from outside, and daily grooming is required to prevent mats from forming. The hair needs to be clipped or tied up away from the eyes so that the dog can see clearly

Utility

Alaskan Malamute

affectionate • friendly • loyal • devoted • aloof • dignified • stubborn

SIZE 58–71 cm (23–28 in) • WEIGHT 38–56 kg (85–125 lb) • COAT Thick, coarse guard topcoat with dense undercoat • COLOUR Light grey through intermediate shadings to black, or gold through shades of red to liver, always with white on underbody, parts of legs, feet and part of mask markings
• LIFESPAN 12 years

Working

Alaskan Malamutes are strong, powerful and have plenty of stamina. They are affectionate, but also aloof, independent and unresponsive to requests unless there is something in it for them. Friendly and easy-going with humans, they need plenty of socialization to stay tolerant of other dogs.

ORIGINALLY BRED to pull sleds in Antarctica.

Special characteristics
The Alaskan Malamute is a dog with great stamina and power.

Exercise requirements
High. Needs a great deal of exercise.

Attitude to
OWNERS affectionate but not demonstrative
CHILDREN good if raised with them
OTHER PETS good if raised with them
STRANGERS aloof
UNFAMILIAR DOGS can be problematic

Perfect owner
Active, energetic owner who will be able to find an outlet for this dog's excess energy.

Potential problems
Tends to be aggressive towards other dogs, and may be aggressive over food.

⚠ This dog's thick coat means that it may overheat in the summer. Owners should be prepared for loose hair around the house.

Beauceron

versatile • bold • calm • courageous • biddable

SIZE 63–70 cm (25–27½ in) • WEIGHT 30–39 kg (66–85 lb) • COAT Short, rough and thick • COLOUR Black and tan • LIFESPAN 11–13 years • In the 'Miscellaneous' class in the USA

Beaucerons are calm, discerning, dependable and hard working with plenty of energy. They are strong, playful and protective, and need adequate socialization with people and other dogs when young.

ORIGINALLY BRED to herd and guard livestock.

Attitude to

OWNERS affectionate, protective
CHILDREN good if raised with them
OTHER PETS good if raised with them
STRANGERS friendly if well socialized
UNFAMILIAR DOGS friendly if well socialized

Perfect owner
Experienced, strong-willed, active owner who can provide this intelligent dog with a job to do as well as plenty of games, activity and socialization.

Potential problems
May be aggressive to strangers if inadequately socialized.

Working

Special characteristics
This active and protective dog has a double dewclaw on its hind legs.

Exercise requirements
High. Enjoys plenty of activity.

Bernese Mountain Dog

confident • good-natured • friendly • courageous • protective

SIZE **58–70 cm (23–27½ in)** • WEIGHT **40–44 kg (87–90 lb)** • COAT Medium length, soft, silky with bright natural sheen • COLOUR Tricolour • LIFESPAN **8–9 years**

Working

Good-natured and strong, Bernese Mountain Dogs are wilful and protective and need kind but firm ownership. In the right hands, they are friendly, happy and outgoing.

ORIGINALLY BRED to pull carts.

Special characteristics
Strong and protective.

Exercise requirements
Medium. Enjoys exercise and play.

Attitude to
OWNERS affectionate, loyal
CHILDREN good if raised with them
OTHER PETS good if raised with them
STRANGERS good if well socialized
UNFAMILIAR DOGS good if well socialized

Perfect owner
Experienced, strong-willed, physically strong, easy-going owner who can give this dog plenty of socialization, exercise and play.

Potential problems
Dogs from some lines may display territorial aggression and other aggression problems.

⚠️ The loose jowls of this breed lead to saliva control problems.

Greater Swiss Mountain Dog

confident • good-natured • friendly • courageous • protective

SIZE 60–72 cm (23½–28½ in) • WEIGHT 59–61 kg (130–135 lb) • COAT Short, dense, glossy • COLOUR Tricolour • LIFESPAN 10–11 years

Strong and larger than the Bernese, Greater Swiss Mountain Dogs have a strong, protective nature. If well socialized, they are happy, gentle giants, but care needs to be taken with other dogs.

ORIGINALLY BRED to pull carts.

Special characteristics
Strong and protective.

Exercise requirements
Medium. Enjoys exercise and play.

Attitude to
OWNERS affectionate, loyal
CHILDREN good
OTHER PETS good
STRANGERS good if well socialized
UNFAMILIAR DOGS can be problematic

Perfect owner
Experienced, physically strong, easy-going owner who can give this dog plenty of socialization, exercise and play.

Working

Bouvier des Flandres

wilful • amiable • calm • sensible • protective

SIZE 59–68 cm (23–27 in) • WEIGHT 27–40 kg (59–88 lb) • COAT Abundant, coarse, thick • COLOUR Fawn, black, brindle • LIFESPAN 11–12 years • In the 'Herding' class in the USA

Working

Strong and robust enough to drive cattle and pull carts, Bouvier des Flandres have a strong personality to match. They can be wary of strangers, territorial and problematic with other dogs unless well socialized and in the care of strong-willed owners.

ORIGINALLY BRED to herd cattle and pull carts.

Special characteristics
This active and protective dog likes to chase.

Exercise requirements
Medium.

Attitude to
OWNERS affectionate, loyal
CHILDREN good if raised with them
OTHER PETS good if raised with them
STRANGERS wary, territorial
UNFAMILIAR DOGS can be problematic

Perfect owner
Experienced, strong-willed, physically strong owner who has time and energy to train, socialize, play games, groom and exercise these powerful dogs.

Potential problems
Tends to be aggressive to strangers and other dogs unless properly socialized.

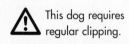 This dog requires regular clipping.

Boxer

playful • exuberant • inquisitive • devoted • outgoing • agile • strong

SIZE 53–63 cm (21–25 in) • WEIGHT 25–32 kg (55–70 lb) • COAT Short, glossy, smooth • COLOUR Fawn or brindle with white markings • LIFESPAN 10–12 years

Boxers are exuberant, energetic, playful and agile. They are good-natured and friendly to all, although proper socialization is needed to ensure they are tolerant of other dogs.

ORIGINALLY BRED to hang on to the nose of large game until hunters arrived.

Special characteristics
The Boxer is tenacious, agile and playful.

Exercise requirements
High. Loves to do everything at speed.

Attitude to
OWNERS affectionate, devoted
CHILDREN playful, exuberant (may be too much for very young children)
OTHER PETS good if raised with them
STRANGERS friendly if well socialized
UNFAMILIAR DOGS can be problematic unless well socialized

Perfect owner
Experienced, active, affectionate families who will enjoy an exuberant, responsive dog and who have enough time and energy for exercise, play and training.

Potential problems
Tends to be aggressive to unfamiliar dogs unless well socialized.

⚠ This dog's shortened nose can make breathing difficult, and it is likely to snore. Their loose jowls can lead to a lack of saliva control.

Working

Bullmastiff

powerful • reliable • alert • loyal • stubborn

SIZE 61–69 cm (24–27 in) • WEIGHT 41–59 kg (90–130 lb) • COAT Short and hard • COLOUR Any shade of brindle, fawn or red with black muzzle • LIFESPAN 10 years

Working

Powerful and strong, Bullmastiffs require training and owners need physical strength if they are to stay in control. These dogs do not require very much exercise considering their large size, but they need careful socialization with other dogs to remain tolerant.

ORIGINALLY BRED as a guard dog.

Special characteristics
The Bullmastiff is protective, strong and independent.

Exercise requirements
Low – Medium. Enjoys exercise but not over-demanding.

⚠️ This dog's shortened nose can make breathing difficult, and it is likely to snore. Loose jowls can lead to lack of saliva control.

Attitude to
OWNERS affectionate, loyal
CHILDREN protective, can knock over small children
OTHER PETS good if raised with them
STRANGERS reserved unless well socialized
UNFAMILIAR DOGS can be problematic unless well socialized

Perfect owner
Experienced, physically strong, strong-willed owner who will socialize and train this powerful dog well.

Potential problems
Tends to be aggressive to other dogs and to strangers unless well socialized.

Canadian Eskimo Dog

alert • active • enduring • strong • independent • aloof

SIZE 50–70 cm (19½–27½ in) • WEIGHT 18–40 kg (40–88 lb) • COAT Thick, dense undercoat with hard, stiff guard hairs • COLOUR Any • LIFESPAN 12–13 years

Canadian Eskimo Dogs are energetic, independent hunters. Reserved and aloof with strangers, they have a strong pack instinct and readily take on other dogs over food or territory. They are scavengers and will hunt, chase and kill smaller pets.

ORIGINALLY BRED to pull sleds in the Canadian Arctic.

⚠️ This dog needs daily grooming to prevent mats from forming in its thick coat. It will overheat easily in summer, so care needs to be taken in the warmer months.

Special characteristics
This active dog has plenty of stamina.

Exercise requirements
High. Enjoys working (hunting or pulling sleds).

Attitude to
OWNERS affectionate, independent
CHILDREN best in adult households
OTHER PETS may kill small pets and chase
STRANGERS reserved, aloof
UNFAMILIAR DOGS can be problematic

Perfect owner
Experienced, strong-willed, active owner who wants a dog to work with them, either sled-pulling or hunting.

Potential problems
Tends to be aggressive to other dogs, both unfamiliar and within the household, and to display aggression over food and territory.

Working

Dobermann

bold • responsive • alert • strong-willed • loyal • obedient

SIZE 65–69 cm (25½–27 in) • WEIGHT 30–40 kg (66–88 lb) • COAT Smooth, short and glossy • COLOUR Definite black, brown, blue or fawn only, with rust-red markings • LIFESPAN 12 years • ALSO KNOWN AS Doberman Pinscher

Working

Dobermanns are strong in both body and mind. Easily trained, they make natural guards and are affectionate and loyal to their owners. They have abundant energy and they need careful socialization when young.

ORIGINALLY BRED to guard.

Perfect owner
Experienced, strong-willed, active owner who will socialize and train this powerful dog and find time to play, exercise and keep it occupied.

Potential problems
Dogs from some lines may be aggressive to strangers and other dogs. May display status-related aggression to gentle owners.

Special characteristics
Strong-willed and protective.

Exercise requirements
High. Needs a great deal of exercise.

Attitude to
OWNERS affectionate, loyal
CHILDREN natural guard
OTHER PETS good if raised with them
STRANGERS reserved, territorial
UNFAMILIAR DOGS can be problematic
unless well socialized

Giant Schnauzer

bold • alert • reliable • calm • inquisitive • eager • persistent

SIZE 60–70 cm (23½–27½ in) • WEIGHT 32–35 kg (70–77 lb) • COAT Harsh, wiry with dense undercoat
• COLOUR Pure black or pepper and salt • LIFESPAN 11–12 years

Exuberant and strong-willed, Giant Schnauzers are inquisitive and persistent. They are responsive, playful and protective towards owners. Barking is a favourite hobby and they make excellent watchdogs.

ORIGINALLY BRED to herd and guard cattle.

Special characteristics
This alert and playful dog is a natural guard.

Exercise requirements
Medium.

Attitude to
OWNERS affectionate, loyal
CHILDREN natural guard
OTHER PETS good when raised with them
STRANGERS guarding, territorial
UNFAMILIAR DOGS can be problematic

Perfect owner
Experienced, active, strong-willed, affectionate owner who can give this active dog a job to do.

Potential problems
Tends to display excessive territorial barking, and status-related aggression to gentle owners.

Working

⚠ The coat needs daily brushing to keep it tangle-free and also requires regular clipping.

Great Dane

alert • powerful • exuberant • outgoing • independent

SIZE 71–76 cm (28–30 in) • WEIGHT 46–54 kg (100–120 lb • COAT Short, dense and sleek • COLOUR Brindle, fawns, blue, black, harlequins (white with black patches) • LIFESPAN 8–10 years

Working

Great Danes are large and exuberant. They tend be clumsy and may knock delicate things flying. Usually they are gentle giants, but care should be taken to train and socialize them early as bad behaviour can be very dangerous in a dog of this size.

Attitude to
OWNERS affectionate, independent
CHILDREN good if raised with them, may knock young children over
OTHER PETS good if raised with them, may chase
STRANGERS friendly if well socialized
UNFAMILIAR DOGS friendly if well socialized

Perfect owner
Experienced, physically strong, strong-willed owner who will socialize this dog well and have homes and cars large enough to accommodate this giant.

Potential problems
Dogs from some lines may be aggressive to people and to other dogs.

ORIGINALLY BRED to hunt large game.

Special characteristics
The Great Dane is inquisitive, exuberant and playful.

Exercise requirements
Medium – High. Enjoys exercise but can be quiet at home.

Greenland Dog

alert • active • enduring • strong • independent • aloof

SIZE 51–68 cm (20–27 in) • WEIGHT 27–47.5 kg (60–105 lb) • COAT Impenetrable undercoat, with outer coat of coarser longer hair • COLOUR Any • LIFESPAN 13 years

Greenland Dogs are very energetic and need a job to do. Their hunting instincts are strong and they should not be trusted with small pets. Reserved and aloof with strangers, they are likely to be difficult with other dogs unless controlled.

ORIGINALLY BRED to pull sleds in the Arctic.

Special characteristics
This active dog has plenty of stamina and loves to hunt.

Exercise requirements
High. Enjoys working (hunting or sled-pulling).

Attitude to
OWNERS affectionate, independent
CHILDREN best in adult households
OTHER PETS may kill small pets and tends to chase
STRANGERS reserved, aloof
UNFAMILIAR DOGS can be problematic

Perfect owner
Experienced, strong-willed, active owner who wants a dog to work with them, either pulling a sled or hunting.

Potential problems
Tends to be aggressive to other dogs, both unfamiliar and within the household, and to display possessive aggression.

Working

Hovawart

watchful • agile • self-assured • playful • alert • biddable

SIZE **58–70 cm (23–27½ in)** • WEIGHT **25–40 kg (55–88 lb)** • COAT **Medium length, with fine, light undercoat** • COLOUR **Black/gold, gold, black** • LIFESPAN **12–13 years**

Working

Hovawarts look similar to Flat Coated and Golden Retrievers, but are very different in temperament. They make good guards, being naturally alert and protective as well as reserved with strangers. They are playful, responsive and devoted to their owners.

ORIGINALLY BRED to guard homes and livestock.

Attitude to

OWNERS affectionate, devoted
CHILDREN good if raised with them
OTHER PETS good if raised with them
STRANGERS reserved, territorial
UNFAMILIAR DOGS friendly if well socialized

Perfect owner
Experienced, active owner who will socialize this dog well and provide it with plenty of activity, games and exercise.

Potential problems
Dogs from some lines tend to be aggressive to other dogs and to strangers.

Special characteristics
The Hovawart is alert and protective.

Exercise requirements
Medium. Does not demand a great deal of exercise.

Leonberger

amenable • friendly • self-assured • playful

SIZE 65–80 cm (25½–31½ in) • WEIGHT 34–50 kg (75–110 lb) • COAT Medium length with evident mane at throat and chest • COLOUR Lion gold, red, reddish-brown, sandy (fawn or cream), always with a black mask • LIFESPAN 9–11 years

Leonbergers are playful, good-natured and energetic. Since Newfoundlands played a part in their ancestry, they also like to swim.

ORIGINALLY BRED to resemble the lion on the Coat of Arms of the Town Hall of Leonberg, Germany.

Special characteristics
Friendly and playful, the Leonberger likes to swim.

Exercise requirements
Medium. High when young.

Attitude to
OWNERS affectionate, loyal
CHILDREN good if raised with them, may knock small children over
OTHER PETS good if raised with them
STRANGERS friendly if well socialized
UNFAMILIAR DOGS friendly if well socialized

Perfect owner
Experienced, active, affectionate, physically strong owners who will have plenty of time to socialize puppies and for activity, play, training and exercise when older.

Potential problems
Dogs from some lines may be aggressive to strangers and to other dogs.

Mastiff

powerful • courageous • calm • affectionate • protective

SIZE **70–76 cm (27½–30 in)** • WEIGHT **79–86 kg (175–190 lb)** • COAT **Short** • COLOUR **Apricot-fawn, silver-fawn, fawn, or dark fawn-brindle. Muzzle, ears and nose should be black with black around orbits, and extending upwards between them** • LIFESPAN **9–10 years**

Working

Powerful and courageous, the Mastiff's sheer size alone would deter all but the most determined intruder. They are protective of owners and territory and require a great deal of time for early and continued socialization with both dogs and people.

ORIGINALLY BRED for guarding.

Attitude to

OWNERS affectionate, loyal

CHILDREN protective, can knock over small children

OTHER PETS good if raised with them

STRANGERS reserved unless well socialized

UNFAMILIAR DOGS can be problematic unless well socialized

Perfect owner

Experienced, physically strong, strong-willed owner who will socialize and train this powerful dog well and who has a large home and car to accommodate this giant breed.

Potential problems

Dogs from some lines may be aggressive to strangers and other dogs, and may show status-related problems.

Special characteristics

The Mastiff is alert and protective.

Exercise requirements

Low – Medium. Enjoys exercise without being over-demanding.

⚠️ This dog's shortened nose can make breathing difficult, and it is likely to snore. Loose jowls will lead to saliva control problems.

Neapolitan Mastiff

powerful • devoted • loyal • protective • courageous

SIZE 65–75 cm (25½–29½ in) • WEIGHT 50–70 kg (110–154 lb) • COAT Short, dense, with good sheen
• COLOUR Preferred black, blue, all shades of grey, brown varying from fawn to red • LIFESPAN 9–11 years
• In the 'Miscellaneous' class in the USA

Slow and ponderous, Neapolitan Mastiffs are friendly, calm and devoted to their owners. They are protective of owners and territory and require a great deal of time for early and continued socialization with both dogs and people.

ORIGINALLY BRED to guard livestock, later for dog-fighting.

Special characteristics
This dog is alert and protective.

Exercise requirements
Low – Medium.

Attitude to
OWNERS affectionate, loyal
CHILDREN protective, can knock over small children
OTHER PETS good if raised with them
STRANGERS reserved unless well socialized
UNFAMILIAR DOGS can be problematic unless well socialized

Perfect owner
Experienced, physically strong, strong-willed owner who will socialize and train this powerful dog well and who has a large home and car to accommodate this giant dog.

Potential problems
Dogs from some lines may be aggressive to strangers and other dogs, and may show status-related problems.

⚠ This dog's shortened nose can make breathing difficult, and it is likely to snore. Loose jowls will lead to problems of saliva control.

Working

Newfoundland

devoted • gentle • docile • calm

SIZE **66–71 cm (26–28 in)** • WEIGHT **50–69 kg (110–152 lb)** • COAT Medium length, with thick undercoat • COLOUR **Black, brown, Landseer (white with black markings)** • LIFESPAN **9–11 years**

Working

Newfoundlands love to swim and will try to rescue anyone from the water whether they are in trouble or not. Their thick coat can make them uncomfortable in summer or in heated houses. Calm and gentle, they need early training and socialization because of their large size.

ORIGINALLY BRED to help fishermen by hauling in nets and pulling carts.

Special characteristics
The playful Newfoundland loves to swim.

Exercise requirements
Medium. Prefers to exercise in water.

Attitude to
OWNERS affectionate, devoted
CHILDREN good if raised with them, may knock over young children
OTHER PETS good if raised with them
STRANGERS friendly if well socialized
UNFAMILIAR DOGS friendly if well socialized

Perfect owner
Experienced, physically strong, strong-willed owner who has enough space at home and in the car for these giant dogs and who can provide games and exercise, especially if it involves water.

Potential problems
Dogs from some lines may be aggressive to strangers.

⚠ May overheat in summer. Will require regular brushing to keep coat in good condition. Loose jowls can lead to saliva control problems.

Pinscher (German)

lively • alert • courageous • tenacious • docile • biddable

SIZE 43–48 cm (17–19 in) • WEIGHT 11–16 kg (23–35 lb) • COAT Short, dense, glossy • COLOUR All solid colours from fawn to stag red. Black and blue with reddish/tan markings • LIFESPAN 12–14 years

Energetic, inquisitive and tenacious, German Pinschers are also responsive and biddable. They are unlikely to back down in a fight and need proper socialization with other dogs to prevent problems.

ORIGINALLY BRED to hunt and kill mice and rats.

Special characteristics
This dog is feisty and playful, with an inquisitive nature.

Exercise requirements
High. Needs to burn off energy.

Attitude to
OWNERS affectionate, loyal
CHILDREN good if raised with them
OTHER PETS may kill small pets
STRANGERS friendly if well socialized
UNFAMILIAR DOGS can be problematic unless well socialized

Perfect owner
Experienced, active, strong-willed owner who has time to socialize, train and play with this energetic and lively dog.

Potential problems
May display status-related aggression to gentle owners.

Working

Portuguese Water Dog

energetic • self-willed • courageous • loyal • responsive

SIZE 43–57 cm (17–22½ in) • WEIGHT 16–25 kg (35–55 lb) • COAT Profuse and long • COLOUR Black, white, brown • LIFESPAN 12–14 years

Working

Friendly and playful, Portuguese Water Dogs need plenty to do to use up their energy. Originally, the hair on their legs and part of the tail was clipped to reduce the drag while they were swimming.

ORIGINALLY BRED to help fishermen.

Special characteristics
This playful dog loves being in water.

Exercise requirements
High. Full of energy and adores exercise, especially swimming.

Attitude to
OWNERS affectionate, devoted
CHILDREN good, can be too exuberant for young children
OTHER PETS good if raised with them
STRANGERS friendly if well socialized
UNFAMILIAR DOGS friendly if well socialized

Perfect owner
Active, energetic owner who enjoys grooming and who will find plenty of time for activities, play and exercise to keep this exuberant dog occupied.

Potential problems
May be destructive if under-exercised.

⚠️ This dog's profuse coat requires regular grooming to prevent mats from forming, and regular clipping. Show breeders clip the coat on the back legs and tail, but there is no need for pet owners to do this.

Rottweiler

bold • courageous • confident • calm • biddable • protective

SIZE 58–69 cm (23–27 in) • WEIGHT 41–50 kg (90–110 lb) • COAT Short, thick and glossy • COLOUR Black with clearly defined markings • LIFESPAN 11–12 years

Rottweilers are strong, active and reluctant to show their feelings. They are naturally protective and make powerful, determined guards. They are playful, responsive and affectionate with owners and require early training and socialization.

ORIGINALLY BRED to drive cattle and guard.

Special characteristics
The Rottweiler is protective and courageous, but not very demonstrative.

Perfect owner
Experienced, strong-willed, affectionate owner who has plenty of time to train, play with and exercise this large, powerful dog.

Potential problems
Dogs from certain lines may display aggression to strangers, and status-related aggression problems with gentle owners.

Exercise requirements
High.

Attitude to
OWNERS affectionate, loyal
CHILDREN good if raised with them
OTHER PETS good if raised with them
STRANGERS aloof, territorial
UNFAMILIAR DOGS friendly if well socialized

Working

Russian Black Terrier

independent • courageous • calm • stubborn

SIZE **63–75 cm (25–29 in)** • WEIGHT **40–65 kg (88–143 lb)** • COAT **Short-haired and long-haired varieties. Harsh topcoat with thick woolly undercoat** • COLOUR **Black** • LIFESPAN **10–11 years** • ALSO KNOWN AS **Black Russian Terrier** • **In the 'Miscellaneous' class in the USA**

Working

Strong-willed and tenacious, Russian Black Terriers need experienced owners. Their drive to work and hunt is strong and they need require early and continued socialization with humans and other dogs to stay tolerant.

ORIGINALLY BRED to be a guard/patrol dog for prison, police and army.

Special characteristics
This dog is active and alert.

Exercise requirements
High. Needs to work, but calm at home.

Attitude to
OWNERS **loyal, affectionate**
CHILDREN **natural guard**
OTHER PETS **may kill small pets, may injure cats unless raised with them**
STRANGERS **reserved, suspicious**
UNFAMILIAR DOGS **can be problematic**

Perfect owner
Experienced, strong-willed active owner who can control and take care with this powerful dog as well as provide it with a job to do or plenty of exercise, games and training to keep it occupied.

Potential problems
Tends to be aggressive to strangers and to display status-related aggression to owners.

⚠ This dog's coat requires regular clipping and grooming.

Siberian Husky

active • eager • friendly • gentle • alert • outgoing • independent

SIZE 51–60 cm (20–23½ in) • WEIGHT 16–27 kg (35–60 lb) • COAT Thick, medium length with soft, dense undercoat • COLOUR Any • LIFESPAN 11–13 years

Friendly and outgoing, Siberian Huskies are built for running. Since they are independent with a strong desire to hunt, they can only be let off the lead in secure areas. Owners need to be prepared to run or cycle several miles with this active breed every day as well as giving daily grooming sessions.

ORIGINALLY BRED to pull sleds.

Special characteristics
This husky likes to run great distances, and to chase.

Exercise requirements
High. Full of energy and loves to exercise.

⚠ These dogs will leave loose hair in the house. Their thick coat requires daily grooming to keep it in good condition.

Attitude to
OWNERS affectionate, independent
CHILDREN good if raised with them
OTHER PETS may be problematic with small pets, may chase
STRANGERS friendly if socialized
UNFAMILIAR DOGS friendly if socialized

Perfect owner
Active, energetic owner who will be able to run or cycle with their dog for several miles every day.

Potential problems
May display control problems on walks – may run off and not return. If under-exercised, may be destructive, dig and escape.

Working

St Bernard

steady • kind • courageous • trustworthy • benevolent

SIZE 61–71 cm (24–28 in) • WEIGHT 50–91 kg (110–200 lb) • COAT Short, dense, thick • COLOUR Orange to red with white patches • LIFESPAN 8–10 years

Working

St Bernards are steady, reliable, very large and heavy. Affectionate and loyal to owners, they are naturally protective, and early training and socialization is required.

ORIGINALLY BRED to haul carts.

Special characteristics
This dog is strong and protective.

Exercise requirements
Low – Medium. Not very demanding.

Attitude to
OWNERS affectionate, loyal
CHILDREN good if raised with them
OTHER PETS good if raised with them
STRANGERS territorial unless well socialized
UNFAMILIAR DOGS friendly if well socialized

Perfect owner
Experienced, physically strong, strong-willed owner who has time to socialize these powerful dogs and who has enough space at home and in the car to accommodate their large size.

Potential problems
Dogs from some lines may be aggressive and display status-related problems with gentle owners.

Loose jowls often lead to lack of saliva control.

Tibetan Mastiff

powerful • affable • aloof • courageous • protective • independent

SIZE **61–66 cm (24–26 in)** • WEIGHT **64–82 kg (140–180 lb)** • COAT **Long, thick topcoat, with heavy undercoat** • COLOUR **Rich black, black and tan, brown, various shades of gold, grey and blue; grey and blue and tan** • LIFESPAN **10–11 years**

Courageous and independent, Tibetan Mastiffs are easy-going and calm. Reserved with strangers, they are loyal and protective towards their owners and territory. Early socialization and training is essential for these gentle giants.

ORIGINALLY BRED **to guard livestock.**

Special characteristics
This is a strong and protective dog.

Exercise requirements
Medium. Enjoys exercise.

Attitude to
OWNERS **affectionate, independent**
CHILDREN **natural guard**
OTHER PETS **good if raised with them**
STRANGERS **reserved, territorial**
UNFAMILIAR DOGS **can be problematic**

Perfect owner
Experienced, strong-willed owner who has the time to socialize this large dog and the space to exercise it adequately and safely.

Potential problems
Tends to be aggressive to other dogs. May be aggressive to strangers unless properly socialized.

⚠️ This dog will leave loose hair in the house. Its thick coat needs daily grooming to prevent mats from forming.

Working

Summary

Breed	Size	Exercise	Grooming	Max. life expectancy	Suitable home	Good with children	Good with other dogs	May be allergy friendly
Affenpinscher	○	◭	■	14	T	✓		
Afghan Hound	●	◭	■	14	T	✓	✓	
Airedale Terrier	●	◭	■	13	T	✓		
Akita	●	◭	□	12	T			
Alaskan Malamute	●	◭	□	12	C	✓		
American Cocker Spaniel	◐	▲	■	14	T	✓	✓	
American Eskimo Dog	○	▲	■	13	C	✓	✓	
American Staffordshire Terrier	●	▲	□	12	T			
American Water Spaniel	●	▲	■	14	C	✓		
Anatolian Shepherd Dog	●	△	□	11	C			
Australian Cattle Dog	●	▲	□	12	C			
Australian Shepherd	●	▲	□	13	C	✓	✓	
Australian Silky Terrier	○	▲	■	14	T		✓	
Australian Terrier	○	▲	■	14	T	✓		
Basenji	●	◭	□	12	T	✓	✓	
Basset Fauve de Bretagne	◐	▲	□	14	T	✓	✓	
Basset Griffon Vendeen (Grand)	●	▲	□	12	C	✓	✓	
Basset Griffon Vendeen (Petit)	○	▲	□	12	T	✓	✓	
Basset Hound	◐	◭	□	12	T	✓	✓	
Beagle	◐	▲	□	13	T	✓	✓	
Bearded Collie	●	▲	■	13	T	✓	✓	
Beauceron	●	◭	□	13	C	✓	✓	
Bedlington Terrier	◐	▲	■	15	T	✓	✓	✓
Belgian Shepherd Dog (Groenendael)	●	▲	■	13	T	✓		
Belgian Shepherd Dog (Laekenois)	●	▲	■	13	T	✓		
Belgian Shepherd Dog (Malinois)	●	▲	■	13	T	✓		
Belgian Shepherd Dog (Tervueren)	●	▲	■	13	T	✓	✓	
Bergamasco	●	△	□	12	C			
Bernese Mountain Dog	●	▲	■	9	T	✓		
Bichon Frise	○	△	■	14	T	✓	✓	✓
Black and Tan Coonhound	●	▲	□	12	T	✓	✓	
Bloodhound	●	△	□	10	C	✓	✓	
Bolognese	○	△	■	14	T		✓	
Border Collie	●	▲	■	14	C	✓	✓	
Border Terrier	○	▲	□	14	T	✓	✓	
Borzoi	●	▲	■	13	C		✓	
Boston Terrier	◐	▲	□	13	T	✓	✓	
Bouvier des Flandres	●	◭	■	12	T	✓	✓	
Boxer	●	▲	□	12	T	✓		
Braque Italian (Bracco)	●	▲	□	13	C	✓	✓	
Briard	●	◭	■	12	T	✓	✓	
Brittany	●	▲	■	15	C	✓		
Bull Terrier (English)	●	◭	□	13	T	✓		
Bull Terrier (Miniature)	◐	◭	□	13	T	✓		
Bulldog	○	△	■	9	T	✓		
Bullmastiff	●	△	□	10	T			
Cairn Terrier	◐	▲	■	15	T	✓		
Canaan Dog	●	◭	□	13	T	✓	✓	
Canadian Eskimo Dog	●	▲	■	13	C			
Cavalier King Charles Spaniel	◐	◭	■	11	T	✓	✓	
Cesky Terrier	◐	◭	■	14	T	✓	✓	
Chesapeake Bay Retriever	●	▲	□	13	C			
Chihuahua (Longhaired)	○	△	□	18	T		✓	
Chihuahua (Smooth Coated)	○	△	□	18	T		✓	✓
Chinese Crested (Hairless)	◐	△	■	15	T		✓	
Chinese Crested (Powder Puff)	◐	△	■	15	T		✓	
Chow Chow	●	△	□	12	T			
Clumber Spaniel	●	▲	□	13	C	✓	✓	
Cocker Spaniel (English)	◐	▲	■	14	T	✓	✓	
Collie (Rough)	●	△	■	13	T			
Collie (Smooth)	●	△	□	13	T			
Curly Coated Retriever	●	▲	□	13	C	✓	✓	
Dachshund (Long Haired)	○	△	■	16	T	✓	✓	
Dachshund (Miniature Long Haired)	○	△	■	16	T	✓	✓	
Dachshund (Miniature Smooth Haired)	○	△	□	16	T	✓	✓	
Dachshund (Miniature Wire Haired)	○	△	□	16	T	✓	✓	
Dachshund (Smooth Haired)	○	△	□	16	T	✓	✓	
Dachshund (Wire Haired)	○	△	□	16	T	✓	✓	
Dalmation	●	▲	■	12	T	✓		
Dandie Dinmont Terrier	○	△	■	16	T	✓	✓	
Deerhound	●	△	■	11	C	✓	✓	
Dobermann	●	▲	□	12	T			
Elkhound	●	▲	■	13	T	✓		
English Setter	●	▲	■	13	T	✓		
English Springer Spaniel	●	▲	■	14	T	✓	✓	
English Toy Terrier (Black and Tan)	○	◭	□	13	T		✓	
Estrela Mountain Dog	●	△	□	12	C			
Field Spaniel	●	▲	■	13	C	✓	✓	
Finnish Lapphund	●	▲	□	12	T	✓	✓	
Finnish Spitz	●	▲	■	13	C	✓	✓	
Flat Coated Retriever	●	▲	□	13	T	✓	✓	
Fox Terrier (Smooth)	◐	▲	□	14	T	✓		
Fox Terrier (Wire)	◐	▲	□	14	T	✓		
Foxhound (English)	●	▲	□	11	C	✓	✓	
French Bulldog	○	△	■	12	T	✓		
German Shephard Dog (Alsatian)	●	▲	■	13	T	✓		
German Shorthaired Pointer	●	▲	□	16	C	✓	✓	
German Spitz (Klein)	○	△	■	15	T			
German Spitz (Mittel)	◐	△	■	14	T			
German Wirehaired Pointer	●	▲	■	12	C	✓	✓	
Giant Schnauzer	●	▲	■	12	T			
Glen of Imaal Terrier	◐	▲	□	14	T	✓		
Golden Retriever	●	▲	■	13	T	✓	✓	
Gordon Setter	●	▲	■	14	C	✓	✓	
Grand Bleu de Gasgogne	●	▲	□	14	T	✓	✓	
Great Dane	●	▲	□	10	T	✓	✓	
Greater Swiss Mountain Dog	●	▲	■	11	C	✓		
Greenland Dog	●	▲	□	13	C			
Greyhound	●	△	□	12	C	✓	✓	
Griffon Bruxellois (Brussels Griffon)	○	△	■	14	T		✓	

Size: ○ small ◐ medium ● large   Exercise requirements: △ minimal ◭ average ▲ high

Summary

	Size	Exercise	Grooming	Max. life expectancy	Suitable home	Good with children	Good with other dogs	May be allergy friendly
Hamiltonstövare	●	▲	□	13	C	✓	✓	
Harrier	●	▲	□	12	C			
Havanese	○	△	■	14	T	✓	✓	
Hovawart	●	▲	◧	13	T	✓	✓	
Hungarian Kuvasz	●	▲	■	13	C			
Hungarian Puli	●	▲	□	13	T			
Hungarian Vizsla	●	▲	□	14	C	✓	✓	
Ibizan Hound	●	▲	□	12	C	✓	✓	
Irish Red and White Setter	●	▲	□	13	C	✓	✓	
Irish Setter	●	▲	◧	13	C	✓	✓	
Irish Terrier	●	▲	◧	13	T	✓		✓
Irish Water Spaniel	●	▲	■	13	C	✓	✓	
Irish Wolfhound	●	△	◧	10	C	✓	✓	
Italian Greyhound	◐	△	□	14	T	✓	✓	
Italian Spinone	◐	▲	◧	14	C	✓	✓	
Jack Russell Terrier	○	▲	◧	18	T	✓		
Japanese Chin	○	△	■	13	T			
Japanese Shiba Inu	◐	▲	■	13	T	✓		
Japanese Spitz	◐	▲	■	12	T	✓	✓	
Keeshond	●	▲	■	14	T	✓	✓	
Kerry Blue Terrier	●	▲	◧	14	T			✓
King Charles Spaniel	○	△	□	12	T			✓
Komondor	●	▲	□	12	C			
Kooikerhondje	◐	▲	◧	13	T	✓		
Labrador (Black and Yellow)	●	▲	□	13	T	✓	✓	
Labrador (Chocolate)	●	▲	□	13	T	✓	✓	
Lakeland Terrier	◐	▲	◧	14	T	✓	✓	
Lancashire Heeler	○	▲	□	13	T	✓	✓	
Large Munsterlander	●	▲	◧	13	T	✓	✓	
Leonberger	●	▲	■	11	C	✓	✓	
Lhasa Apso	○	△	■	14	T	✓		
Lowchen	◐	△	■	14	T	✓		
Lurcher	●	▲	◧	14	T	✓	✓	
Maltese	○	△	■	14	T	✓	✓	✓
Manchester Terrier	●	▲	◧	14	T	✓	✓	
Maremma Sheepdog	●	▲	■	12	C			
Mastiff	●	△	□	10	C			
Miniature Pinscher	○	▲	□	14	T			✓
Neapolitan Mastiff	●	▲	□	11	C			
Newfoundland	●	▲	◧	11	C	✓	✓	
Norfolk Terrier	◐	▲	◧	14	T	✓	✓	
Norwegian Buhund	●	▲	◧	15	T	✓	✓	
Norwegian Lundehund	○	△	□	12	T	✓	✓	
Norwich Terrier	○	▲	■	14	T	✓	✓	
Nova Scotia Duck-tolling Retriever	●	▲	□	13	T	✓	✓	
Old English Sheepdog	●	▲	■	13	T	✓	✓	
Otterhound	●	▲	◧	12	C	✓	✓	
Papillon	○	△	■	14	T	✓		
Parson Russell Terrier	◐	▲	◧	14	T	✓	✓	
Pekingese	○	△	■	13	T			✓
Pharoah Hound	●	▲	□	14	C	✓	✓	
Pinscher (German)	●	▲	□	14	T	✓		
Plott Hound	●	▲	◧	13	T	✓		
Pointer	●	▲	□	14	T	✓	✓	
Polish Lowland Sheepdog	●	▲	◧	14	T	✓	✓	
Pomeranian	○	△	■	15	T			
Poodle (Miniature)	◐	▲	■	15	T		✓	✓
Poodle (Standard)	◐	▲	■	13	T	✓	✓	✓
Poodle (Toy)	○	△	■	15	T		✓	✓
Portugese Water Dog	◐	▲	◧	14	T	✓	✓	✓
Pug	○	△	◧	14	T	✓	✓	
Pyrenean Mountain Dog	●	△	◧	11	T			
Pyrenean Sheepdog	●	▲	■	13	T	✓	✓	
Rhodesian Ridgeback	●	▲	□	12	T	✓	✓	
Rottweiler	●	▲	□	12	T	✓	✓	
Russian Black Terrier	●	▲	■	11	T			
St Bernard	●	△	■	10	T	✓	✓	
Saluki	●	▲	□	12	C	✓	✓	
Samoyed	●	▲	■	12	T	✓	✓	
Schipperke	◐	▲	◧	13	T	✓		
Schnauzer (Miniature)	◐	▲	◧	14	T	✓	✓	
Schnauzer (Standard)	●	▲	◧	14	T	✓	✓	
Scottish Terrier	◐	▲	◧	14	T	✓		
Sealyham Terrier	◐	▲	◧	14	T	✓		
Segugio Italiano	●	▲	□	13	C	✓	✓	
Shar Pei	●	▲	□	11	T	✓		
Shetland Sheepdog	◐	▲	■	14	T			
Shih Tzu	○	△	■	14	T	✓	✓	
Siberian Husky	●	▲	◧	13	C	✓	✓	
Skye Terrier	○	▲	■	13	T	✓		
Sloughi	●	▲	□	12	C			✓
Soft Coated Wheaten Terrier	◐	▲	◧	14	T	✓		
Spanish Water Dog	●	▲	◧	14	C			✓
Staffordshire Bull Terrier	◐	▲	◧	12	T			
Sussex Spaniel	◐	▲	◧	12	T	✓	✓	
Swedish Lapphund	●	▲	◧	13	T	✓	✓	
Swedish Vallhund	◐	▲	□	14	T	✓		
Tibetian Mastiff	●	▲	■	11	T			
Tibetian Spaniel	○	△	■	14	T	✓	✓	
Tibetian Terrier	●	▲	■	14	T	✓	✓	
Toy Fox Terrier (American Toy Terrier)	○	△	□	14	T	✓		
Weimaraner	●	▲	□	13	T	✓	✓	
Welsh Corgi (Cardigan)	◐	△	□	14	T	✓	✓	
Welsh Corgi (Pembroke)	◐	▲	□	14	T	✓	✓	
Welsh Springer Spaniel	●	▲	□	14	T	✓	✓	
Welsh Terrier	◐	▲	◧	14	T	✓		
West Highland White Terrier	○	▲	◧	14	T	✓	✓	
Whippet	●	△	□	14	T	✓	✓	
Wirehaired Pointing Griffon	●	▲	■	15	T	✓	✓	
Yorkshire Terrier	○	▲	■	14	T			✓

Grooming: □ weekly or less ◧ frequently ■ daily   Suitable home: C country T town or country

Credits

The author and publisher would like to thank the following people, who kindly allowed us to photograph their dog for this book.

Gundogs

p52 Sentune Acquaro at Bonario 'Riley'/Mrs Kim Parris
p53 Patouche Ultime Reve Avec Bremalyn 'Reva'/Lynne Hawtree
p54 Lutra Easy Dollar 'Sophie'/Mr JR Novis
p55 Hollutrix Abbizia 'Oscar'/Mrs JE Ingram
p56 Kylecroft Countryman Tallis/Mrs Sheila Rees and Mrs GE Breen
p57 Show Champion Blitzan Rhine (Blitzan Kennel)/Ali Cabbledick
p58 Mokelassoc de Ubrique for Hollutrix (imp) 'Ramon'/Gaynor Berry
p59 Lex Terrea/Miss Kate Bull
p61 Anniezu Rocketman (Jago)/Miss Q Rixon
p62 GSP Pipperoo Sven Sandursson 'Diesel'/Mrs P and Miss H Taylor
p63 Kimmax Kennedy 'Kenny'/Mrs W Oxman
p64 Nunneywood Onancock Reed 'Reed'/Mr and Mrs Woods
p65 Gamesmere Royal Escort 'Hugo'/Mrs CE Payne
p66 Telsmoss Mattias JW 'Charlie'/Mr Chris Woolner
p67 Tenfield Border Rambler JW SGWC 'Tor'/Mrs Kim Ellis
p68 Lembas Moonlight Sonata 'Lunar'/JA White
p70 Newfanova Nordic Rhapsody at Ladakhnova 'Saskia'/Mrs J Parker
p71 Piper and Hetty/Alan and Jenny Day
p72 Ecameadow Dark Rider 'Hogan'/Anthony Burke
p73 Maesffynnon Sirius 'Jethro'/Roy Harris
p74 Rustasha Rare Vision via Kerrabi 'Daisy'/Mrs Magaret Pitman
p75 Cottonsocks Choc Waves 'Chocky'/Mrs L and Miss C Prior
p77 Sharemead O'Connor 'Conner'/Mrs Carol Share-Jones
p78 Anbrook Debutanta 'Freya' and Oxwell Once in a Lifetime 'Chase'/Mrs A Drew and Mrs S Brookshaw
p79 (left to right) Rhiwlas Woodcock at Soberhill/K and CD Smith, Sh Ch Dubldee Silk n' Lace/Mrs UG Mosedale, Mishules Geordi La Forge/Shula M Shipton
p80 Foulby Beachcomber at Kerry Kew 'Danny'/Mrs Patricia Neal
p81 Niriti Red Admiral 'Murphy'/Mrs K Kenyon
p82 Fallen Leaf New Kid in Town 'Henley'/Mr and Mrs Cunliffe
p83 Pennylock Ivor of Clynewood 'Dai'/Lesley Breeze

Hounds

p84 Kabella Heaven Knows 'Alice'/Mrs AR Allan
p85 Jiving Jasper 'Jasper'/Jane Addis
p86 Chilton Faites Jos Jeux 'Gamble'/Mick and Jackie Hawkins
p87 Delacroix Helen's Boy with Diamondice 'Merlin'/Mr and Mrs Cutler
p88 Cliffmere Skillful 'Emmy'/Mrs V and Misses MJ and RJ Longman
p89 Ch. Weatheroak Inspiration of Barleycliffe 'Milo' and Trailfinder Beloved Fabien of Barleycliffe 'Fabien'/Mr O'Keefe
p91 'Glow'/Mrs J Newsham

p92 Melminds Melly Mel/Melanie Chapman
p93 Barnaby Rudge 'Barnaby'/Miss B Spooner
p94 Ch. and Irish Ch. Emem Nipper in the Air/Mandy Dance
p95 Dixie Dreamer/Mrs JE Pierce
p96 Bardachs Santana/Mr and Mrs Lewis
p97 Cempsey Coquet JW 'Jessica' and Siluae Zloty at Cempsey 'Lotty'/Mr and Mrs Gordon
p98 Ch Kilbourne Celtic at Hammonds/Mrs A Randall
p99 Steldawn Rainsong/Ms C Walker
p100 Ch Toveri Arvokas/Mrs J Bateman and Mr and Mrs Burne
p101 Dazzleby Darter, Dazzleby Daydream and Dazzleby Daring/Mrs R Griffiths
p102 Kantilou Passion 'Claudia'/Mr and Mrs Parker
p103 Sulamin Stop the Calvelry 'Ben'/Sue Pearce
p104 Lazy Maize 'Maizy'/Sue Bolden
p105 Tedandi Destiny's Child/Mrs A Jowers
p107 Chahala Cheetah 'Cheetah'/Mrs A Wilde
p108 Ballyphecan Bridget at Boscaleanb 'Bridget'/Mr and Mrs Box
p112 Ankors Behutet/Antony Bongiovianni
p114 Nyuki Mask of Zorro/Sara-Lea Davies
p115 Tasia Elouise/Mrs E Metcalfe and Mr MJ Green
p116 Chahala Otto 'Otto'/Jenny Startup
p117 Falconcrag Zaa Faran of Akhanubis/Maria Teresa Contessa de Cesare
p118 Welstar As You Like It at Monelli 'Mabel'/Miss E Burgess

Pastoral

p119 Tuzla 'Adi'/Remzi Mustafa
p121 Ozzypools Wild Rover 'George'/Mrs Glynis Dowson
p122 Damalier Dream Come True 'Skye'/Mrs S Hudson
p123 SR Sabrefield Raring To Go 'CDEX'/T P Davis
p124 Belkanti Love Token at Donnieland/Hilary Jones
p126 Kelluki Angelic Whisper 'Indi'/Mrs LJ Hatcher
p127 Chique Adulation 'Baggio'/Valerie Röttger
p128 Troumerle Denim at Jepanil/J Barker and P Young
p130 Morvania Funky Monkey 'Titan'/Miss TL Morrison
p131 Manordeifi Silver Dawn/Mrs DJ Moores
p132 Asterel Sir Lancelot/Trisha Dean
p133 Fin Ch. Lumiturpa Pigga at Elbereth/Toni Jackson
p136 Rockisland Lap of Luxury at Sinergi 'Purdey'/Mr and Mrs Colledge
p138 Colnestar Jailhouse Rock at Audaxus/Mrs Judith Spooner
p139 Ch. Oceano Atlantic Della Collina de Revigliasco de Sunhaze/Mrs S. Hewart-Chamber
p140 Champion Rikarlo Skylark from Jumasue/Mr and Mrs Purves and JA Hearson
p141 Meisan Summer Sensation 'BB'/Sandra Wilson
p142 Szafir/Val Smith
p143 Ch. Oceano Atlantico della Collina de Revigliasco de Sunhaze and Ch. Abraccadarbra della Sunhaze

Credits

Index

Index

Acknowledgements

Special photography
Steve Gorton and Angus Murray

Animal Photography/Sally Anne Thompson 106, 229.
Ardea/John Daniels 137, 163.
Corbis UK Ltd 48.
John Daniels 14 left, 39, 43, 109, 110, 125, 135, 144, 147,
157, 162.
DK Images 60, 111, 113, 203, 221, 227, 233.
Frank Lane Picture Agency/J & C Sohns 8.
Octopus Publishing Group Limited 9, 16/Rosie Hyde 17, 22
Top, 27 top, 40, 44, 45 /Ray Moller 22 bottom, 23, , 69
bottom, 129, 134, 153, 158, 161, 166, 169, 172, 181, 205

bottom, 236, 245 /
Ironbark Australian Cattle Dogs/Angela Cocker
www.ironbarkacd.co.uk 120.
The Kennel Club/David Dalton 152, 241.
RSPCA Photolibrary/Angela Hampton 41 /Tim Sambrook 47.
Marsha Shively/e-mail: wish360@aol.com 200.
Vom Treuen Freund/Malin Jones www.malinjones.com
www.geocities.com/hovawartdogs/index.html 238.
Warren Photographic/Jane Burton 2-3, 25 bottom.
Wave Crest American Water Spaniels/Lara A Suesens
http://wavecrestaws.tripod.com 42, 76.
WyEast Kennels/Jim & Kathy Corbett
www.anypet.com/dog/wyeast.html (tel: ++1 503 649 2712)
90 left, 90 right.

Executive Editor **Trevor Davies**
Project Editor **Jessica Cowie**
Executive Art Editor **Leigh Jones**

Design **Louise Griffiths**
Picture Research **Luzia Strohmayer**
Assistant Production Controller **Aileen O'Reilly**